WORDS ON THE WILDERNESS

A HISTORY OF PLACE NAMES
IN
SOUTH FLORIDA'S NATIONAL PARKS

LARRY PEREZ

ECITY • PUBLISHING

To the many authors before me who saw fit to record the details of this area's colorful history – thank you all! Larry Perez

Words on the Wilderness;
A History of Place Names in South Florida's National Parks

Copyright © 2007 text by Larry Perez, All Rights Reserved.

Requests for permission to reproduce material
from this work should be sent to:
larryperez@wordsonthewilderness.com

Cover Art & Design by Larry Perez & Joy Brunk
Cover Photos courtesy of Florida State Archives, Joy Brunk, Quan Dong, Allyson Gantt
Cover Map from istockphoto.com
Cover Photo of author courtesy of Tammie Bondonzi Perez

Set in Times New Roman 11/14pt

Printed and Bound in the U. S. A.

First Edition, First Printing, October 2007

ISBN 978-0-9716006-5-2

ECITY • PUBLISHING
P O Box 5033
Everglades City, FL, 34139
mrepko@earthlink.net
telephone (239) 695-2905

More South Florida books from this publisher:
  A Brief History of the Everglades City Area
  The Story of Everglades City; A History for Younger Readers
  Historia de Everglades City
  Frog Poop & other Stories

Table of Contents

Acknowledgements — iii
Introduction — 1

Chapter 1: Big Cypress National Preserve — 3
   Geographic Features — 5
   References — 23

Chapter 2: Biscayne National Park — 27
   Geographic Features — 29
   References — 47

Chapter 3: Dry Tortugas National Park — 51
   Geographic Features — 53
   References — 59

Chapter 4: Everglades National Park — 61
   Structures and Facilities — 63
   Geographic Features — 69
   References — 137

Further Reading — 151
Photo Credits — 153

Acknowledgements

In a book about names, its only appropriate to drop a few that were instrumental in helping me complete this text. To the following individuals I owe a tremendous debt of gratitude for their inspiration and support. In no particular order they are:

Roger Hammer, Castellow Hammock Nature Center
Fred & Sandy Dayhoff, Loop Road Royalty
Nancy Russell, Jenny Barton, Kate Dahl-Kerney, Katherine Fleming and the entire Everglades Collections staff
Mike Ryan, Fort Pulaski National Monument
Sonny Bass, Everglades National Park
Bill Loftus, Everglades National Park
Bob DeGross, Big Cypress National Preserve
Richard Curry, Biscayne National Park
Brenda Lazendorf, Biscayne National Park
Bob Showler, Biscayne National Park
Beryl Given, Everglades Association
Jim Clupper, Islamorada Public Library
Dr. Paul George, Miami-Dade College
Captain Franklin Adams, Naples
The staff of the Collier County Museum
The staff of the Miami Dade Public Main Library

I would like to express my deepest thanks to my editor, Marya Repko, for her boundless enthusiasm and appreciation for the value of this work.

Finally, about my wonderful wife, Tammie, and my two incredible children, Kylic and Drake, I cannot say enough. Over the years, you've given me both endless inspiration and unconditional support. Thank you for understanding why Daddy felt the need to spend so many hours in front of the computer and so much time hidden away in the big library downtown!

Introduction

Nearly two years ago, I began what I though would be a simple and straightforward task: figure out the origins of place names in Everglades National Park. As a ranger, I had staffed the park's visitor center for countless hours and had spent quite a bit of time pouring over maps of the area. Every lake, river, bay, island, campsite and road had a name, though where they came from was often not readily apparent. Some were humorous, some were foreboding and others were simply intriguing. In my spare time, I began to casually pen a list of these monikers and their background stories.

It wasn't long after I began that I realized the tales of the Everglades were inextricably linked to the stories of our other South Florida national parks. Long before we established political boundaries between them, these areas were one; hosting the migration of countless characters between them. During the course of my research, I slowly began documenting the origins of names in the Big Cypress, Biscayne Bay, and the Dry Tortugas. Scarcely realizing it, my project had doubled in size.

Numerous writers have penned accounts of the better-known dramas in South Florida history. Because many such stories took place in the theater of these parks, documentation tracing the history of our more prominent nomenclature was easy to find. But in the wake of these familiar names remained a plethora of colorful monikers with no discernible explanation. Written resources were scarce, and hearsay and oral accounts were often all that remained to tell the tale. I committed myself to always finding the most reliable account available and documenting the source of my findings. My casual, part-time project had suddenly turned into a full-fledged academic paper.

Throughout college, I struggled to produce the requisite 10-page reports on philosophy, sociology, and chemistry. Thus, to be able to present to you this publication marks a significant personal accomplishment. Yet despite my pride and joy for the book you are now holding, I must confess a little secret: this book does not tell the whole story.

INTRODUCTION

This book was meant to serve as a tool for those interested in the cultural and natural history of South Florida. Throughout the text, I have given only a brief narrative of the events that unfolded in these locations. Others have written about them far more eloquently than I ever could, and I have been careful to cite these authors should you wish to read more.

The text does not cover every possible place name to be encountered in our South Florida parks. Due to the enormity of this project, I felt the need to limit myself to only those locations specifically noted on visitor maps. An abundance of lesser-known locations do exist, and are arguably just as compelling as those contained herein. But for the mere sake of preserving my sanity, I have only included here 445 individual accounts.

Libraries, interviews, and archives yielded only partial information on a number of the monikers in question. In these circumstances, evidence was carefully reviewed to attain plausible explanations. For these entries, the text reflects the author's best possible guess.

In a select number of instances, little or no information could be secured to explain the nomenclature of an area, and as you will find, I have not been shy to admit it. Thus, it is important for the reader to understand that this book has not been written in stone. Rather, this publication is a work in progress. I look forward to continuing my research and hearing from those who may be able to point me in the right direction. I dedicate this work to the community of South Florida, which has provided me with so much over the years, and I hope in turn, that the community will assist me in preserving their proud and unique history.

Questions, comments and suggestions may be sent to the author at:
LarryPerez@wordsonthewilderness.com

Chapter 1

BIG CYPRESS NATIONAL PRESERVE

In the heart of southwest Florida lies a 750,000-acre preserve known as Big Cypress. Since its protection in 1974, this vast mosaic of water and land has beckoned countless visitors to marvel at its unique ecology. But long before its designation as a national preserve, this landscape served as the stage for a compelling drama of human perseverance.

The history of Big Cypress is a rich complex of diverse human experience set amidst a rugged, untamed wilderness. It is a shared story of perseverance across cultural divides; a narrative of human achievement over the inhospitable forces of nature. It is the story of countless African-American and Hispanic-American workers who labored in the fertile agricultural fields and logging mills of the region. It is the story of Florida's "crackers" – cowmen who successfully raised cattle here amidst less than favorable conditions. It is the story of countless fishermen and hunters who, over the course of centuries, sought subsistence, recreation and fortune from the verdant landscape. It is the story of man's ingenuity in traversing this landscape atop uniquely engineered vehicles. It is the story of countless laborers, toiling under extreme conditions towards the completion of the Tamiami Trail. It is the story of military men who scoured this landscape in the heat of war against the Seminoles. It is the story of the countless Native Americans who sought refuge here and their progeny who still dwell on these lands today.

Today, the Big Cypress seeks to preserve many of the same traditional uses it has afforded man in the past. It seeks to do so in a fashion that also guarantees those opportunities in perpetuity. As a national preserve, rather than a national park, it provides a chance for individuals to forge their own experiences among the swamps in the foreseeable future.

The map for Big Cypress reveals 61 distinctly named places with the boundaries of the preserve. Many serve to commemorate important people, places, or events that helped shape the preserve's unique identity. An examination of these helps reveal the finer details of this story.

Big Cypress

At one time in South Florida's history, this area might have been called "Big Cypress" for the size of the trees which grew here. However, during the early 20th century, most of the old growth in the area was cleared for lumber.[1]

Present-day visitors to the park walk among the relatively young progeny of these ancient trees. The National Park Service reminds visitors that the preserve's moniker refers to the size of the landscape rather than that of the individual trees.[2]

Much of the Big Cypress is in Collier County which was established in 1923 and named after Barron Gift Collier, a streetcar advertising mogul who bought up over 1 million acres in southwest Florida and spearheaded the completion of the Tamiami Trail (US-41) through the Big Cypress.

Oasis Visitor Center

You can find more information about Big Cypress at the center which is about 50 west of downtown Miami on US-41 (Tamiami Trail). The Oasis Visitor Center started life in the late 1960s as a private airport with a hangar and restaurant. The facility became a recognizable landmark owing to a large airplane perched atop the eatery as decoration.[3] It was bought by the National Park Service in the early 1980s.

GEOGRAPHIC FEATURES

Airplane Prairie
This vast prairie boasts a large, smooth, open area where hunters would land small planes to bring in supplies and fly out their wild game. It is thought that a drug plane crashed there, probably in the early 1970s, but the name pre-dates that incident.[4]

Bamboo Slough
The term "slough" (pronounced "slew") is used regionally to denote any low-lying area of land that serves to channel slow-moving water. This particular slough is no doubt named for the profusion of blue maidencane, *Amphicarpum muhlenbergianum*, which is found growing there.[5]

Bear Island Campsite
Florida black bear, *Ursus americanus floridanus*, are found in the Everglades and Big Cypress region, though in fewer numbers than were formerly present.[6]

Birdon Road (CR-841)
This odd moniker is actually a contraction of the names of two area entrepreneurs. H. W. Bird and J. F. Jaudon built a tomato packing plant by the same name along this road in the early 1930s.[7] The farming and packing industries here gave rise to a sizeable settlement of laborers by the same name. Though this ephemeral town was to disappear by the late 1940s, the road still retains the same intriguing label.[8]

Burns Lake Campsite
This body of water derives its name from John and Mary Burns, homesteaders that settled in the area around 1959 or 1960. They are remembered as an affable couple that would grade the road to their property by dragging a large blade behind their old tractor. They operated a small sawmill here until 1971 and snaked logs on the road that would also come to bear their name.[9]

BIG CYPRESS NATIONAL PRESERVE

Burns Road
This roadway takes travelers to a lake of the same name. The road was constructed during the widening of US-41 in 1958 for access to the Burns Lake excavation.[10]

California Slough
As early as the late 1800s, there existed an old Seminole camp by the name of "Californee" in the vicinity of the headwaters of this slough. It served as the home site for Billy Fewel (otherwise known as "Key West" Billie). Why the camp bore this name is difficult to determine, but rest assured we are not the first to wonder.[11] In 1918, a survey party happened upon the impoverished camp. A member of this party would later suggest that perhaps the Seminoles had seen the name on a can of California fruit at a store or trading post, and adopted it as their own.[12]

Coconut Hammock
This moniker is derived from the stand of tall coconut palms that have been planted upon the island. The site once served as the Tigertail Trading Post, though today it is privately owned.[13]

Copeland Prairie
This prairie lies just east of a town by the same name. Both honor David Graham Copeland, a key figure in the completion of the Tamiami Trail. After a career in the Navy during World War I,[14] he was hired as chief engineer for the building of the Trail and also took care of Barron Collier's other interests.[15] Copeland was Chairman of the Collier County Board of Commissioners from 1929 until 1947 when he was elected to the Florida State House of Representatives. He died in 1949.

Mrs. John Briggs, Sr., wife of Barron Collier's chauffeur, once relayed this testament to his character, "You know what Mr. Copeland did for us every Christmas? He would put up a huge Christmas tree. There were a lot of poor people down there and he saw that everybody got a present. Also, everybody that worked for him got a turkey or ham. Its no wonder the town of Copeland was named for him."[16]

BIG CYPRESS NATIONAL PRESERVE

Concho Billy Trail
This area served at one time as the encampment of a deaf and mentally-retarded Indian of the same name.[17]

Cow Bell Strand
Though select areas of the Big Cypress have historically been used for cattle ranching, no evidence seems to exist to explain the origins of this unique place name.

Dade-Collier Training and Transition Airport
As air traffic increased during the 1960s, the Dade County Port Authority began to scout for a location to expand operations. Ideally, they hoped to find an area that could service both the East and West coasts. In 1968, this site was selected and construction promptly began. Thirteen million dollars were invested in the project, $740,000 of which was provided by the Federal Aviation Administration. The Jetport was to be constructed in phases, with the first being only those structures necessary for conducting training operations. Later phases would convert the field into a full-service airport for cargo and passenger craft. By 1970, however, overwhelming public concern over potential environmental impacts scuttled plans for any further expansion.[18]

Dayhoff Slough
This slough is named for Fred and Sandy Dayhoff, long-time employees of the National Park Service for both Everglades National Park and Big Cypress National Preserve. They have lived on a two-and-a-half acre parcel of property on Loop Road for the nearly 45 years.

Sandy once recounted how many of the place names in the Big Cypress were derived from the individuals who either hunted the areas or opened up the country for others.[19] Such was the case for this slough, as it was where the Dayhoffs did the majority of their hunting and trapping prior to the preserve's establishment. Though the Dayhoffs knew the area informally as "Limpkin Valley", the United States Geological Survey gave it the current moniker on the advice of locals.[20]

Deep Lake Strand

This strand is named for the lake it harbors. The lake is aptly named, as it is among the few in the Everglades / Big Cypress region that reaches profound depths. It has been recounted that at one time this lake was anywhere from 90 to 130 feet deep.[21,22] Several accounts relay the existence of tarpon in the lake, a fact which leads some to believe that this "bottomless lake" actually bears a conduit to the coast. At one time, the area was a busy community as both a citrus grove and packing house in the Collier empire.[23]

Dixons Slough

This slough was likely named for Earl Dixon, a local who owned a hunting camp off Loop Road.[24] He was a frogger who frequented the slough that bears his name. He was remembered by some for providing improvements, at his own expense, to the airboat landing that lead to this waterway.[25]

Doctor's Prairie

Known by some as "The Doctor", this prairie seems to have been christened for an Indian who resided in the area during the early 1900s. Evidence suggests this may have been a Seminole by the name of Grover Doctor.[26] The Indian reputedly maintained six or seven hundred head of cattle on the prairie and cultivated a large number of crops on a large hammock nearby. The latter has also been referred to as "Doctors Hammock".[27]

Dr Tiger Hammock

This island receives its name for an Indian medicine man by the same name. Dr Tiger (photo) lived on this hammock with his family in the late 1890.[28]

East Crossing Strand

It is currently unclear why this particular strand has been so named. While it might be assumed that the area served as a travel route, it is not know who may have traversed it, when it may have been used, or where they were headed.

BIG CYPRESS NATIONAL PRESERVE

East Hinson Marsh
Exactly who, or what, this name serves to commemorate remains a mystery. No evidence exists to suggest how this marsh derived its current moniker.

Fire Prairie Trail
As the recipient of more lightning strikes than any other area of North America, wildfire is a natural component of the South Florida ecosystem. The haphazard burning of our natural areas creates a mosaic of habitats that foster the growth and persistence of diverse flora and fauna. It is plausible, therefore, that this prairie received its name from one such recent fire.

Florida National Scenic Trail
This pathway is one of only eight designated National Scenic Trails in the country.[29] Its southernmost leg (photo) runs roughly forty-five miles right down the middle of the Big Cypress National Preserve.[30] While this represents some of the most strenuous hiking in the state, it comprises only a small fraction of the nearly 1,000 miles of the current Florida National Scenic Trail.

Fortymile Bend
Part of the Tamiami Trail (US-41) has been designated a Scenic Highway and visitors traveling the historic road can often see why. Long stretches of uninterrupted scenery afford motorists just a hint of the beauty and vastness of the Everglades and the Big Cypress terrain.

Following its completion in 1928, facilities were few and far between along the Trail and landmarks were hard to come by. Frequent travelers used a series of jogs in the road as landmarks to guide them. At one of these, Fortymile Bend, the road veers north west, probably so that the already completed Dade portion could meet the new road in Collier County. The bend is named for the fact that it lies roughly forty miles west of downtown Miami.[31] *See also Monroe Station, Tamiami Trail.*

Gannet Strand

Though afforded Federal protection as an endangered species, the Wood Stork, *Mycteria americana*, is a commonly seen resident of South Florida. These large birds are easily identified by the contrast of their bright white plumage against their bald, dark heads. They are conspicuous not only for their size and appearance, but also for their habit of  congregating in large flocks. The wood stork is fond of freshwater environments and feels quite at home among the cypress sloughs of the Big Cypress.

Over the years, the wood stork has been graced with a plethora of colorful monikers, including the wood ibis, flinthead, ironhead, Spanish buzzard and preacher. It was also referred to frequently as the gannet, [32] and it has been said that those from northern Florida would simply call them "gants".[33] It is probable, therefore, that this strand was christened for a profusion of wood storks that once sought refuge there.

Gator Hook Strand, Gator Hook Swamp

A "gator hook" was a common instrument used by hunters to extract an alligator from his cave or prod the animal to surface.[34] A typical gator hook was little more than a curved piece of metal on a long pole. These tools were frequently used and even served as the namesake to one of the more notorious bars in the historic town of Pinecrest.

Though such hooks were ubiquitous in the area and may have been the inspiration for this place name, an alternate explanation has been suggested. Another popular means of catching alligators involves baiting a large hook on a line in the hopes of attracting a hungry gator. These lines are checked every few days, and it seems plausible that this may have been a popular location for this type of trapping.[35]

Georges Strand

This geographic feature is named for an African-American man named George Cromartie. George lived in the vicinity of this strand with his wife Hattie and their pet pig, Turner.[36]

The Cromarties lost their son to an accident at the local Reynold's Sawmill. A regulatory law of the time allowed the families of mill workers killed on the job to be afforded residence on the site in compensation. The Cromarties continued to live on the site long after the demise of the mill itself.[37]

The Cromartie house was a popular spot for locals. It served as a sort of "jumping off" point for froggers and hunters. It was not unusual to find a number of swamp buggies collected here, as the couple was well-known for their hospitality.[38] When their home burnt during a wild fire in the early 1960s, local hunters and buggy owners helped to build a new cabin.[39]

Gum Slough
Today, would-be adventurers can climb aboard fat-tired swamp buggies and follow trails to rather remote areas of the Big Cypress. But prior to the availability of all-terrain military equipment following World War II, navigating these swamps often entailed venturing out in a modified Model A or Model T Ford. Given the difficulties of the landscape, it was not uncommon to find oneself inextricably stuck in a quagmire of water and muck. This particular slough was known to be extremely soft, and earned its current moniker due to its "gumbo-like" consistency. Probably because of the difficulty of crossing this area, a stand of old-growth pine was spared by loggers and continues to thrive to the south in an area known as Lostmans Pines.[40]

H. P. Williams Roadside Park
This tiny roadside rest area is named for Homer P. Williams, an engineer who worked for Barron Collier during the construction of the Tamiami Trail. This park is believed to be the first of its kind in the State of Florida.[41]

Halfway Creek Canoe Trail
It has been written that this waterway lies, appropriately enough, halfway between Barron River in Everglades City and Turner River at Chokoloskee.[42] The banks were farmed with sugar cane and there was a thriving settlement at the mouth of the creek in the early 1900s.[43]

Hess Hammock
This large tree island was named for Ben Hess, a local hunter who maintained a large campsite on the hammock.[44]

Kirby Storter Roadside Park
This tiny roadside rest area honors Kirby S. Storter, a member of one of the area's pioneering families. For several years, Storter worked as a carpenter and electrician for Barron Collier and later oversaw construction of South Florida roads (including the Tamiami Trail) as a project engineer for the Florida Road Department. The Florida Legislature designated this park in his honor in 1971, just six years after his retirement.[45]

Kissimmee Billy Strand
One can be sure that this strand is christened for an Indian by the same name. While some writings do exist about a Kissimmee Billy[46], the author has been unsuccessful in uncovering evidence to link the individual to this particular strand.

Loop Road
Otherwise known as State Road 94, this thoroughfare is so named for the "loop" it forms in conjunction with the Tamiami Trail (US-41). Originally constructed in the 1920s by the Chevelier Corporation, the project was an attempt to divert construction of the Tamiami Trail to intersect Chevelier holdings.[47] At its own expense, the Corporation constructed seven miles of road stretching between Fortymile Bend and the small community of Pinecrest. The investment did not payoff, however, as the State legislature opted for a more northerly route. The seven-mile stretch was subsequently deeded to the state, which eventually completed the 22-mile loop to Monroe Station.[48] *See also Pinecrest.*

Lostmans Pines
This large, isolated stand of pines is located near the southernmost boundary of the preserve. It is most likely named for its proximity to Lostmans Slough and the headwaters of Lostmans River. *See also Lostmans River in Everglades National Park.*

BIG CYPRESS NATIONAL PRESERVE

Lostmans Slough
It has been said that this remote area derived its name from the number of misguided individuals who lost their bearings there.[49] However, it is more probable to believe this floodplain of lower elevation is so called because it channels water in a southwesterly direction into Lostmans River. *See also Lostmans River in Everglades National Park.*

Midway Campsite
Those looking for a carnival with rides and games are bound to be disappointed here. This quiet campground is situated along the Tamiami Trail (US-41), and allows campers to spend the night "midway" between Miami and Naples.[50]

Miles City Prairie
The location of Miles City lies squarely within the heart of this prairie. It was named for the youngest son of Barron Collier, the most prominent land developer in southwest Florida. Miles was instrumental in getting President Truman to Everglades City for the opening of the national park. He died of a virus in 954. The area named after him was both a farming and ranching settlement.[51]

Mitchell Landing Campsite
This airboat launch derives its current moniker from Ed Mitchell, proprietor of the Coconuts Camp, who would use the landing to access his isolated in-holding to the southwest.[52] It remains a popular launch site today.

Monroe Station
Prior to the establishment of the Florida Highway Patrol, a group of officers known collectively as the Southwest Mounted Police were organized to render assistance to motorists in distress along the newly completed Tamiami Trail. Located roughly  ten miles apart, a series of filling stations were constructed to house the officers and dispense gasoline and soft drinks to travelers. Stations were

located at Belle Meade, Royal Palm Hammock, Weaver's Camp, Turner River, Monroe Station and Paolita.[53]

This particular station was situated near the Monroe County line and likely received its name from this fact.[54] The county, in turn, is named for James Monroe.[55] During his presidency (1817-25), Monroe would come to acquire the new territory of Florida from Spain.[56]

While most of these stations (and their localities) have since disappeared from the map, Monroe Station was operated privately as a popular wayside restaurant until it was bought by the preserve. Although it has since fallen into disrepair and is closed to visitors, the National Park Service plans to restore the building which is listed on the National Register of Historic Places. *See also Forty Mile Bend, Tamiami Trail.*

Monroe Strand
This strand was likely named for its proximity to the Monroe County line or Monroe Station itself.

Monument Lake Campsite
The namesake for this area can be found right at the entrance to the campground. On February 22, 1936, the Governor of Florida and his cabinet were joined here by David Graham Copeland (representing Collier County) and 273 Seminoles. The meeting was arranged by Governor David W. Sholtz in an effort to ascertain how he could better serve this reclusive population. The Indians' reply was simple and direct, "Just leave us alone."

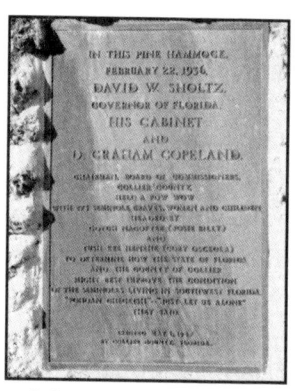

To commemorate both the location and outcome of the meeting, a bronze plaque was cast and a small monument was erected in 1947.

The original plaque was stolen in the 1950s.[57] A replacement was ordered and erected within an elaborate stone wall enclosure across the road from the original monument. While the stone structure still persists, this second plaque has also been stolen. The memorials remain unadorned by bronze but they still serve as poignant reminders of a painful and difficult past.[58]

Mullet Slough

Though mullet are seldom found this far inland today, long-time residents remember finding these adaptable fish in the area.[59] Unlike the free-flowing, uninterrupted wetland of yesteryear, today's Everglades have been divvied up by scores of canals, levees, and water-control structures. The resulting fragmentation of the landscape has brought about many changes, including alterations to the former range of many species. It is probable, therefore, that this area earned its moniker for the fish that were once found here.

New River Strand

This strand ultimately connects with New River, though why this waterway is so named remains a mystery.

Ochopee

James T. Gaunt is credited with naming this now-defunct community along the Tamiami Trail. Gaunt planted roughly 250 acres of tomatoes here in 1928. Following their initial success, farming operations grew considerably. Segregated quarters were soon constructed to house the black and white field laborers. Homes were built across the canal  for the burgeoning Gaunt family and their associates. The community would eventually come to boast a packing house, general store, post office, utility plant, and community garbage collection.

    A number of Seminole Indians lived in the vicinity of Gaunt's fields. They would often work as day laborers or make purchases at the general store. Gaunt would come to recall how Charley Tommy, a regular to the store, helped give rise to the town's unusual moniker. Gaunt once asked Charley how to say "field" in the Seminole language. Charley replied "O-chopp-ee", which Gaunt proceeded to christen the town.

    At its peak, the town of Ochopee comprised some 2,000 acres and was populated by roughly 200 permanent residents. Old timers still recall the idyllic lifestyle that was enjoyed in the rural community.

    Sadly, a catastrophic fire would come to consume most of the town in 1953. In the aftermath, an ad-hoc post office was established in a small tool shed. While Ochopee never really recovered, the tool shed remains to this day (see photo). It has become a popular roadside curiosity, and is often billed as the smallest Post Office in the United States.[60]

Okaloacoochee Slough
It has been written that this name is derived from the Seminole language and means "little bad water", though the exact reason for this designation remains unknown.[61]

Pinecrest Campsite

The Pinecrest campsite, which is situated on the grounds of an old oil well pad, lies near the location of a historic logging community of the same name. Visitors will note that the area is marked by the sudden appearance of pine trees which dominate the landscape. Being some of the tallest trees of the area, they form a visible "crest" above the vegetation, perhaps leading to its current moniker.

In its heyday, Pinecrest was home to between 300 and 400 individuals, and boasted a number of amenities including dormitories, restaurants, bars, casinos, and a shooting range. In addition to logging, residents supplemented their incomes by farming tomatoes, raising chickens, and hunting.

The town had been platted in 1924 (see advertisement) and was to have been a major development until the Tamiami Trial skirted by it.[62]

By 1974, when the area was designated as part of the national preserve, the population was only around 200. With the passage of time, the community has continued to dwindle to only a few residents that currently reside within the Pinecrest area.[63] *See also Loop Road.*

Raccoon Point

The raccoon, *Procyon lotor*, is one of the most ubiquitous mammals in South Florida's natural areas. They are able to adapt to life in a variety of different habitats, including suburbia.[64] As one of the most recognizable of our woodland species, it is only fitting that such an area should bear its name. Yet the question remains: why does this particular locale bear the distinction? The answer will perhaps always remain a mystery. *See also Coon Point in Biscayne National Park, Coon Key in Everglades National Park.*

Roberts Lakes Strand

As with so many tales from the early days of South Florida, two versions of this story persist. While they differ greatly, this much remains certain: sometime between 1896 and 1898, a very lucky Thomas Roberts would come to give his name to this strand and the lake that he happened to find within.

In one version, Roberts was plume hunting in the area, when he happened upon a previously unknown lake teeming with alligators. As skins were fetching a high price at the time, he raced back to Fort Myers to purchase salt to cure the hides. While Roberts was away, another hunter, having found the lake, was also en route to purchase salt at Everglades City. The two parties, returning to the lake at the same time, worked together to fully reap the harvest, which was said to exceed an unlikely 10,000 hides.[65]

Another version has Thomas Roberts working alongside his brother Billie, an accomplished outdoorsman. While on a hunting trip, the pair shot several birds which came to land in a nearby lake. The men were amazed as they watched the fowl disappear, and discovered the lake to be alive with countless alligators. The brothers quickly realized the potential value of their find, but were also aware of the need to utilize an ox cart to haul the bounty from its remote sanctuary.

With no road leading to the lake, they blazed a trail on their way back to Fort Myers. Aware that news of their discovery was spreading, they set to task constructing a truly unique ox cart. The axle was a full foot shorter than most, while the wheels rose higher than most. Upon returning to the lake, the brothers began cutting a narrow path, while leaving fairly tall stumps behind them. Owning the only cart that could successfully navigate the tortuous path, the clever brothers were left to reap a more believable 1,000 hides.[66]

Rock Island Prairie
This prairie may have derived its moniker for a small settlement by the same name. Rock Island is remembered as being little more than a sparse collection of houses and an Atlantic Coast Line Railroad depot.[67]

Seagrape Drive
This short road was almost certainly named for the presence of a particular tree by the same name at some point in time. *See also Sea Grape Point in Biscayne National Park.*

Sig Walker Strand
Walker was a former game warden who maintained a camp and residence on Loop Road. He is remembered for cutting out what would later become Sig Walker's Landing, an airboat trail that would take you south into an open prairie.[68]

Skillet Strand
A hunting camp by the same name formerly existed in the vicinity of this slough. Skillet Camp was once heralded as the farthest outpost of West Coast adventurers. During a short visit here in the midst of blazing the Tamiami Trail, Allen Andrews recounts hearing of a cache of provisions left behind by a previous party.[69] The truth behind this place name may never been known for certain, but it can be believed that one of the items to be left behind at such a camp might have been a heavy cast-iron skillet.

Sweetwater Strand
The drainage for this large strand is focused primarily into Sweetwater Bay. *See also Sweetwater Bay Chickee in Everglades National Park.*

Tamarind Hammock

The wild tamarind, *Lysiloma latisiliquum*, is a common species in the hardwood hammocks of South Florida.[70] It is a member of the legume family and, during our warmer months, boasts flowers reminiscent of a drab mimosa. This tree has gained fame as a favored host of the beautiful liguus tree snails

of the area. The wild tamarind is a Caribbean species and is only found in the United States in South Florida. The current moniker is fitting, as the tamarind remains the most conspicuous canopy tree of this hammock. *See also Tree Snail Hammock Trail.*

Tamiami Trail (US-41)

J. F. Jaudon, a Dade County tax assessor, was a prominent land owner in the Big Cypress area. He eagerly sought the creation of a trans-coastal highway to protect his interests in the Chevelier Corporation, and lobbied to have the Trail routed through his lands in Dade County.[71] See Loop Road, above, to read about his Pinecrest development.

To further this goal, he encouraged journalist William Stewart Hill to write a series of newspaper articles on the benefits that could accrue from such a highway.[72] The effort worked and construction began soon thereafter.

The name is attributed to E. P. Dickey, who suggested the moniker in 1915 at the first meeting of the State Road Department.[73] It is derived from a contraction of the road's two terminals: Tampa and Miami.

The section of road through the Big Cypress was built from 1923 to 1928, thanks to Barron Collier who financed much of the project after Collier County was established. The stone archway pictured above once graced the Dade/Collier County line but was torn down in the late 1950s when the road was widened. *See also Fortymile Bend, Monroe Station.*

BIG CYPRESS NATIONAL PRESERVE

Tree Snail Hammock Trail

This trail is named for the beautiful liguus tree snails of South Florida.[74] Often described as the "jewel of the Everglades", these invertebrates display a wide variety of colors and patterns. They prefer to graze upon the lichens that grow upon the smooth bark of many hammocks trees, most notably the wild tamarind, which dominates the canopy here. *See also Tamarind Hammock.*

Turner River Canoe Trail

In 1857, Captain John Parkhill of the U.S. Army led an expedition of seventy-five men up this waterway in search of Indian encampments. Their guide was Captain Richard Turner, who successfully landed the contingent nine miles up river. While several Indian camps were found, the expedition would ultimately end in tragedy. A scouting party was unexpectedly ambushed, leaving six men, including Captain Parkhill, dead.[75]

Captain Turner would later return to this area to become one of the earliest known white settlers. Turner settled upon the banks of this river around 1874 and lent his name to it.[76]

Wagonwheel Road (CR-837)

Numerous accounts have been written regarding the use of oxen and wagons to traverse the Big Cypress during the dry season.[77] Typically, these carts were used to haul provisions, agricultural crops or the spoil of a successful hunt. One of the largest plantations in the area was that of the Deep Lake Strand, and extensive detail exists regarding the use of oxen at this grove.[78]

It seems plausible that this path may have been one of several used to access the area. It is also easy to imagine that, with the relatively heavy volume of goods that would have forded this challenging terrain, evidence of failed attempts may have been discarded along the path. Perhaps such an item remained long enough to give rise to this road's current moniker.

Windmill Prairie

Evidence suggests that a windmill did, in fact, exist on this prairie at one time.[79] Sadly, it appears the only basis for this are stories from those who remembered the structure. While no details exist about the appearance, owner, or purpose of the mill, the area is remembered as the site of a cattle ranching operation and the structure may have supported this enterprise.[80]

REFERENCES

[1] Tebeau, Charlton W. *Man in the Everglades*. University of Miami Press. Miami, FL. 1968. Pg. 22

[2] National Park Service. *Big Cypress Official Park Map*. Government Printing Office. 496-196/40435. 2003.

[3] National Audubon Society. *The Big Cypress Natonal Preserve, Research Report #8*. National Audubon Society, New York, NY. 1985. Pg. 287.

[4] Captain Franklin Adams, *Personal Commentary*. August 6, 2007.

[5] Wunderlin, Richard P. *Guide to the Vascular Plants of Florida*. University Press of Florida. Gainesville, FL. 1998

[6] Gingerich, Jerry Lee. *Florida's Fabulous Mammals*. World Publications. 1994. Pg. 78.

[7] Repko, Marya. *A Brief History of the Everglades City Area*. ECity Publishing. Everglades City, FL. 2001. Pg. 63.

[8] Jamro, Ron. "Signposts to Nowhere: Collier's First Ghost Towns Linger in Name Only". *Naples Daily News*. Sunday, October 31, 1999.

[9] Doerr, Vince. Oral Interview conducted July 28, 1992. National Park Service. *Big Cypress National Preserve Oral History Collection. Volume 2*. Everglades National Park. Collection BICY #9763

[10] Duever, Michael J., et al. *The Big Cypress National Preserve*. National Audubon Society. New York, NY. 1979. Reprint 1986. Pg. 261.

[11] Glenn, James Lafayette. *My Work Among the Florida Seminoles*. University Presses of Florida. Orlando, FL. 1982. Pg. 70

[12] Andrews, Allen H. *A Yank Pioneer in Florida*. Douglas Printing Co., Inc. Jacksonville, FL. 1950. Pg. 102

[13] Dayhoff, Fred. *Personal Commentary*. February 24, 2004.

[14] Tebeau, Charlton W. *Florida's Last Frontier*. University of Miami Press. Miami, FL. 1957. Pg. 87

[15] Stone, Maria. *The Tamiami Trail: A Collection of Stories*. Butterfly Press. Naples, FL. 1998. Pg. 51.

[16] Stone, Maria. *The Tamiami Trail: A Collection of Stories*. Butterfly Press. Naples, FL. 1998. Pg. 99

[17] Stone, Calvin R. *Forty Years in the Everglades*. Atlantic Publishing Company. Tabor City, NC. 1979. Pg. 69

[18] National Park Service. *Resource Inventory and Analysis of the Big Cypress National Preserve*. 1979.

[19] Dayhoff, Sandy. Oral Interview conducted June 29, 1992. National Park Service. *Big Cypress National Preserve Oral History Collection. Volume 2*. Everglades National Park. Collection BICY #9763

[20] Dayhoff, Fred. Oral interview and airboat tour conducted on February 24, 2004.

[21] Fritchey, John. *Everglades Journal*. Florida Heritage Press. Miami, FL. 1992. Pg. 54.

[22] Dimock, A.W. & Julian A. *Florida Enchantments*. The Outing Publishing Company. New York. 1908. Reprint 1975. Pg. 258.

[23] Stone, Maria. *The Tamiami Trail: A Collection of Stories*. Butterfly Press. Naples, FL. 1998. Pgs. 15, 26

[24] Dayhoff, Sandy. Oral Interview conducted June 29, 1992. National Park Service. *Big Cypress National Preserve Oral History Collection. Volume 2*. Everglades National Park Collection BICY #9763.

[25] Conly, Ruth. Oral Interview Transcripts. National Park Service *Big Cypress National Preserve Oral History Collection. Collection. Volume 2*. Everglades National Park Collection BICY #9763.

[26] Nash, Roy. *Approximate Location of Permanent Seminole Camps*. Map. 1930. U. S. Government Printing Office.

[27] Fritchey, John. *Everglades Journal*. Florida Heritage Press. Miami, FL. 1992. Pg. 18, 86.

[28] Dayhoff, Sandy. Oral Interview conducted June 29, 1992. National Park Service. *Big Cypress National Preserve Oral History Collection. Volume 2*. Everglades National Park. Collection BICY #9763.

[29] United States Forest Service. *Florida Trail Official Map and Guide*. February 2006.

[30] Florida Trail Association. *Florida Trail Big Cypress Fact Sheet*. July, 2006.

[31] Dayhoff, Sandy. Oral interview and tour conducted on September 14, 2004

[32] Kale, Herbert W., II & David S. Maehr. *Florida Birds: A Handbook and Reference*. Pineapple Press. Sarasota, FL. 1990

[33] Fritchey, John. *Everglades Journal*. Florida Heritage Press. Miami, FL. 1992. Pg. 18, 240.

[34] Brown, Loren G. "Totch". *Totch: A Life in the Everglades*. University Press of Florida. Gainesville, FL. 1993. Pg. 166

[35] Dayhoff, Sandy. Oral Interview conducted June 29, 1992. National Park Service. *Big Cypress National Preserve Oral History Collection. Volume 2*. Everglades National Park. Collection BICY #9763.

[36] Dayhoff, Sandy. Oral Interview conducted June 29, 1992. *National Park Service. Big Cypress National Preserve Oral History Collection. Volume 2*. Everglades National Park. Collection BICY #9763

[37] Dayhoff, Sandy. Oral interview and tour conducted on September 14, 2004.

[38] Dayhoff, Sandy. Oral Interview conducted June 29, 1992. National Park Service. *Big Cypress National Preserve Oral History Collection. Volume 2*. Everglades National Park. Collection BICY #9763.

[39] Captain Franklin Adams, *Personal Commentary*. August 6, 2007.

[40] Dayhoff, Fred. Oral interview conducted on May 27, 2005

[41] Mayer, M. A. & Virginia A. Below. *For Your Information: Homer P. Williams Roadside Park*. Collier County Museum. Naples, FL. 1998

[42] Tebeau, Charlton W. *Florida's Last Frontier*. University of Miami Press. Miami, FL. 1957. Pg. 120.

[43] Repko, Marya. *A Brief History of the Everglades City Area*. ECity Publishing. Everglades City, FL. 2001. Pgs. 14, 16.

[44] Dayhoff, Sandy. Oral Interview conducted June 29, 1992. National Park Service. *Big Cypress National Preserve Oral History Collection. Volume 2*. Everglades National Park. Collection BICY #9763.

[45] Mayer, M. A. & Virginia A. Below. *For Your Information: Kirby S. Storter Park*. Collier County Museum. Naples, FL. 1998/2001

[46] Weisman, Brent Richards. *Unconquered People: Florida's Seminole and Miccosukee Indians*. University Press of Florida. August 1999.

[47] Andrews, Allen H. *A Yank Pioneer in Florida*. Douglas Printing Co., Inc. Jacksonville, FL. 1950. Pg. 140.

[48] National Park Service. *Resource Inventory and Analysis of the Big Cypress National Preserve*. Pgs. 751-752. 1979.

[49] Wangerin, G. B. Oral Interview conducted June 24, 1992. National Park Service. *Big Cypress National Preserve Oral History Collection. Volume 2*. Everglades National Park. Collection BICY #9763.

[50] Dayhoff, Sandy. Oral interview and tour conducted on September 14, 2004.

[51] Repko, Marya. *A Brief History of the Everglades City Area*. ECity Publishing. Everglades City, FL. 2001.

[52] Wangerin, G. B. Oral Interview conducted June 24, 1992. National Park Service. *Big Cypress National Preserve Oral History Collection. Volume 3*. Everglades National Park. Collection BICY #9763.

[53] Stone, Maria. *The Tamiami Trail: A Collection of Stories*. Butterfly Press. Naples, FL. 1998. Pgs. 59-60.

[54] Dayhoff, Sandy. Oral Interview conducted June 29, 1992. *National Park Service. Big Cypress National Preserve Oral History Collection. Volume 2*. Everglades National Park. Collection BICY #9763

[55] Bloodworth, Bertha Ernestine. *Florida Place-Names*. University of Florida. August 1959. Pg. 20

[56] Adicks, Richard, editor. *Le Conte's Report on East Florida*. The University Presses of Florida. Orlando, FL. 1978. Pg. 5

[57] Captain Franklin Adams, *Personal Commentary*. August 6, 2007.

[58] Dayhoff, Sandy. Oral interview and tour conducted on September 14, 2004

[59] Captain Franklin Adams, *Personal Commentary*. August 6, 2007.

[60] Stone, Maria. *Ochopee: The Story of the Smallest Post Office*. Butterfly Press. Naples, FL. 1989.

[61] Read, William A. *Florida Place-Names of Indian Origin and Seminole Personal Names.* Louisiana State University Press. Baton Rouge, LA. 1934. Pg. 23.

[62] Captain Franklin Adams, *Personal Commentary.* August 6, 2007.

[63] Dayhoff, Sandy. Oral interview and tour conducted on September 14, 2004.

[64] Gingerich, Jerry Lee. *Florida's Fabulous Mammals.* World Publications. Tampa, FL. 1999. Pg. 80.

[65] Tebeau, Charlton W. *The Story of Chokoloskee Bay Country.* Florida Flair Books. Miami, FL. 1955. Pgs. 47-48

[66] Andrews, Allen H. *A Yank Pioneer in Florida.* Douglas Printing Co., Inc. Jacksonville, FL. 1950. Pgs. 185-187.

[67] Jones, Jr., C. J. Oral Interview conducted July 15, 1994. National Park Service. *Big Cypress National Preserve Oral History Collection. Volume 2.* Everglades National Park. Collection BICY #9763

[68] Wolfe, Ben. Oral Interview conducted 1995. National Park Service. *Big Cypress National Preserve Oral History Collection. Volume 3.* Everglades National Park. Collection BICY #9763.

[69] Andrews, Allen H. *A Yank Pioneer in Florida.* Douglas Printing Co., Inc. Jacksonville, FL. 1950. Pgs. 147

[70] Wunderlin, Richard P. *Guide to the Vascular Plants of Florida.* University Press of Florida. Gainesville, FL. 1998. Pg. 364

[71] Paige, John C. *Historic Resource Study for Everglades National Park.* National Park Service. 1986. Pg. 115

[72] Paige, John C. *Historic Resource Study for Everglades National Park.* National Park Service. 1986. Pg. 113

[73] Tebeau, Charlton W. *Florida's Last Frontier.* University of Miami Press. Miami, FL. 1957. Pg. 221

[74] Close, Henry T. *Liguus Tree Snails of South Florida.* University Press of Florida. December 2000.

[75] Tebeau, Charlton W. *Florida's Last Frontier.* University of Miami Press. Miami, FL. 1957. Pg. 47

[76] Tebeau, Charlton W. *Florida's Last Frontier.* University of Miami Press. Miami, FL. 1957. Pg. 97

[77] Andrews, Allen H. *A Yank Pioneer in Florida.* Douglas Printing Co., Inc. Jacksonville, FL. 1950. Pgs. 185-187

[78] Dimock, A.W. & Julian A. *Florida Enchantments.* The Outing Publishing Company. New York. 1908. Reprint 1975. Pgs. 255-256

[79] Dayhoff, Sandy. Oral Interview conducted June 29, 1992. National Park Service. *Big Cypress National Preserve Oral History Collection. Volume 2.* Everglades National Park. Collection BICY #9763.

[80] Captain Franklin Adams, *Personal Commentary.* August 6, 2007

Chapter 2

BISCAYNE NATIONAL PARK

For visitors arriving by car, there is only one entrance to Biscayne National Park – the Dante Fascell Visitor Center in Homestead. But for those fortunate enough to visit the park by boat, there are an endless array of routes into this jewel of the National Park Service.

Comprised mostly of the warm shallows of Biscayne Bay, roughly 93% of the park is submerged. Visitors explore every nook and cranny of these waters on a daily basis, searching for the perfect game fish, the perfect dive spot, or the perfect place to find a bit of solitude. While the style of boats may have changed, the allure of the Bay has remained the same for thousands of years.

One of the most impressive sights to be found within the park's vast acreage are the living coral reefs that lie just offshore of the barrier islands. Here colorful sea fans sway in the currents while fish of every shape and size dart about in abundance. Creatures from one's dreams may be found dwelling among them. Eels, cuttlefish, sea stars, turtles – more than one could possibly imagine.

While thousands of visitors flock here annually to enjoy their ancient beauty, these same corals proved a treacherous obstacle to mariners not very long ago. Many a ship has foundered upon the shallow reefs, and ample evidence persists to this day of their demise. Reefs through the Florida Keys bear the names of the vessels they scuttled or the mariners who sometimes went down with them.

Glancing at a map of Biscayne National Park, one can find 69 distinctly named locales. Each hints at the maritime history that has unfolded in its depths. European surveyors, rogue pirates, early pioneers, modern legislators and the "Conchs" of the Florida Keys have all left their imprint in the rich nomenclature here.

Biscayne National Park

The true origin of the name "Biscayne" will perhaps never be known, though various explanations do exist. It has been suggested, for example, that early Spanish explorers named these waters for the Bay of Biscay, located just north of Spain.[1] It has also been  said to originate from a man in the area who was referred to as "El Biscaino", from the Spanish province of Biscay.[2]

Still another theory persists. The Tequesta were a collection of aboriginal tribes that inhabited the lower east coast of Florida during Europe's first contact with the "new" world. Despite nearly two and a half centuries of European exploration, only occasional and sporadic accounts exist to give us insight into these long-lost cultures. One account mentions a particular tribe in this group which lived primarily near present day Miami and the nearby islands. For reasons still unclear, the Spanish christened them the "Viscaynos", which in subsequent centuries has been corrupted into the namesake for Biscayne Bay.[3]

Dante Fascell Visitor Center

This visitor center is named for Florida Congressman Dante Bruno Fascell, who served 19 consecutive terms in the United States House of Representatives. From 1954 to 1993, Fascell forged a career in public service that would come to span eight presidential administrations. He earned distinction for his efforts in open government, foreign affairs, and environmental issues.

Honoring his memory though this visitor center is apropos, as his support was instrumental in the creation of Biscayne National Park, Everglades National Park, Dry Tortugas National Park and the Florida Keys National Marine Sanctuary. In 1998, Fascell passed away in Clearwater, Florida, but not before receiving the prestigious Presidential Medal of Freedom from President Bill Clinton.[4]

GEOGRAPHIC FEATURES

Adams Key
Regarding this particular moniker, there are only two facts known for certain. The first is that this island was given its current name in 1854 by the United States Coastal Survey. The second is that the officer that christened this island was Sub-Assistant I. H. Adams.[5] Though not clear whom he intended to honor with this designation, one might assume the officer seized the opportunity to immortalize himself.

Ajax Reef
Originally built in 1826, the vessel *Ajax* had only been in service a decade before she met her demise on this shallow reef. While en route from New York to Mobile with a load of cargo, the 133-foot vessel ran aground here on November 14, 1836.[6]

Alicia Wreck
Carrying a cargo of furniture and trade goods, the Spanish freighter *Alicia* ran aground on Long Reef on April 21, 1905. Salvage attempts were unsuccessful, and the reef remains the final resting ground for this impressive ship. The vessel was built in Glasgow in 1883 and measured a full 345 feet in length.[7]

Anniversary Reef
Biscayne National Park celebrated its twenty-fifth anniversary in 1993. During that year, a variety of events were planned to mark the occasion. For one such event, a delegation of VIPs and dignitaries was invited to join park staff on a guided snorkeling tour.

Park Science Coordinator Richard Curry (third from right in photo) suggested taking the group to a little-known and unnamed reef nearby. The pristine site was a hit among the guests and the area has been known as "Anniversary Reef" ever since![8]

Arsenicker Keys (East, Long, and West Arsenicker)
A number of keys in both Everglades and Biscayne National Parks share this cryptic moniker in some form.

Two stories currently circulate regarding the origins of this name, though neither can likely be verified with any certainty. While I have my personal favorite, I will let the reader decide which is more probable.

It has been suggested that the current moniker is a corruption of "marsh sneaker", the Bahamian term for herons.[9] The term would have had merit given the slow and deliberate manner of hunting employed by these birds. Furthermore, given the Cockney accent with which this term was likely spoken, it is easy to understand how the name evolved over time.

However, it is also commonly known that the eggs of both herons and egrets were harvested for sustenance by the local islanders. Often this would not sit well with the birds, leading them to "nick" the fleeing poachers in the "arse" – the British term for derriere!

Bache Shoal
The Bache name is prominent in United States naval history. Several officers have borne the name, and several ships have, in turn, been named in their honor. Perhaps best known among them was Alexander Dallas Bache who was appointed Second Superintendent of the Coast Survey in 1843 and is largely regarded as the catalyst for the ultimate completion of the monumental task.[10]

During the lengthy efforts of the coastal survey, officers would routinely stumble upon previously unknown (or uncharted) geographic features. These would be christened with arbitrary names, often with little explanation as to who, or what, was being commemorated. But while it might appear this reef suffered the same fate, it seems almost certain that, given his longevity and influence towards the completion of the coastal survey, this shoal pays tribute to Alexander Dallas Bache.

Ball Buoy Reef

Prior to the establishment of Biscayne National Park, a conspicuous marker was placed here to help mariners locate this beautiful reef. A large iron buoy measuring roughly fifteen feet across was tethered to the sea floor in the vicinity.[11]

Although the buoy disappeared following a storm in 1978, its anchor point can still be found. Evidence suggests that these bright orange buoys may have been used to locate other impressive reefs in the area, as similar anchor sites have been located elsewhere.[12]

Billys Point

This jut of land on the ocean side of Elliott Key was named for William D. Albury, one of the first homesteaders in the park. Informally known as "Uncle Billy", Albury served for a time as justice of the peace for the handful of residents in the area, and was known to assist in legal affairs for his neighbors.[13]

Biscayne Channel

This channel cuts through Stiltsville in the northern end of Biscayne Bay near southern Key Biscayne.

Black Ledge

It is currently unclear how this particular place name originated.

Black Point

This spit of land likely derives its name from the fact that it serves as the drainage of the Black Creek Canal. While it is unclear why this historic creek would garner such a moniker, one can surmise it arose from a dark tint in the water. Tannin is commonly leached from the mangroves growing along the shoreline, creating the dark rust-colored water that is so characteristic of the South Florida coast.

Boca Chita Key

It is likely that the original name for this island became corrupted over time. The origins are no doubt Spanish, as the first half of the epithet is easily translated to mean "mouth". Similar names have been used around South Florida, including Boca Grande ("big mouth"), Boca Chica ("small mouth"), and Boca Raton ("mouth of the rat").

The term "Chita", however, has no literal meaning. Given the relative abundance of corruption among the area's nomenclature (i.e., Key Largo, Matecumbe Keys, and Key West), the original name has, in all likelihood, fallen victim to linguistic error.

Bowles Bank

It is possible that this bank was named for famed British loyalist William Augustus Bowles (1763-1805). Bowles boasted a number of exploits in the territory of Florida. He maintained an active relationship with the Creek Indians who sought refuge here, and would eventually come to marry the daughter of a chief by the name of Perryman.

Following the surrender of Florida, it is known that Bowles continued to trade freely with the Seminoles of the lower east coast from a base on the Bahamian Islands.[14]

Brewster Reef

Like so many other reefs along the treacherous Florida Keys, this area is named for the ship that met its demise here in March of 1848. The 700-ton *Brewster* foundered on this reef with a cargo of cotton, hemp, lard and sugar before eventually succumbing to her injuries.[15]

Broad Creek

As its name implies, this is a broad channel that traverses the southern boundary of the park just below Swan Key.

Caesar Creek, Caesar Creek Bank

Black Caesar was one of the most notorious pirates to plunder the eastern seaboard. Several accounts identify the bandit as an African chief of immense size and strength who successfully overpowered the crew of the slave ship that sought to sell him in the new world.

Upon escape, Black Caesar dwelled for some time during the late 17th century on Elliott Key and the nearby islands of Biscayne Bay. It is said that here he amassed a large band of marauders and would assail ships taking riches along the trade route to the old world. The shallow inlets and channels, along with the treacherous reef, afforded Caesar the perfect backdrop for treachery.

It is reputed that the pirates kept prisoners on Elliott Key, as well as a large harem of women taken from plundered ships. Wealth was reportedly accumulated and buried on the island, and to this day treasure seekers are often drawn looking for riches.

In recent years, the validity of many of these claims has been called into question. It is known that in the early 1700s, Black Caesar joined ranks with famed buccaneer Blackbeard (Edward Teach), and ultimately met his fate at the hands of the U.S. Government in September of 1718. However, it is unknown how much of the story of Black Caesar in South Florida is apocryphal.

Still, it is from these stories that the shallow creek which flows between Elliott and Old Rhodes Keys gets its name.[16]

Finally, it is interesting to note that this cut has also been mapped as "Black Sarah's Creek".[17] It is somewhat tantalizing to ponder that this area may also have been named for the exploits of some mysterious female buccaneer.

Christmas Point

Maps identify the southern point of Elliott Key as Christmas Point as early as 1890.[18] Previous efforts to discern the origins of this place name have proven fruitless[19] and it appears the true meaning behind this moniker will perhaps never be known.

Convoy Point

The *Convoy* was a sloop hired for service during the United States Coastal Survey in 1852. Lieutenant Joseph Swift Totten utilized the vessel during his survey of Biscayne Bay that year and no doubt bestowed the name in her honor.[20]

Coon Point

It is telling that the raccoon has bestowed its name upon places in three of the four national parks in South Florida. In fact, this charismatic mammal is so ubiquitous, it is reasonable to question why any one area should deserve this designation. *See also Raccoon Point in Big Cypress National Preserve and Coon Key in Everglades National Park.*

Cutter Bank Shallows

No evidence currently exists to explain this particular place name.

Elkhorn Coral Reef

Elkhorn coral, *Acropora palmate,* is a common branching coral of Caribbean waters.[21] This species grows predominantly on shallow reefs that often experience significant wave action. The resulting breakage and fragmentation is one method of reproduction.[22] Not surprisingly, this reef derives its name for the profusion of elkhorn corals found here.

Elliott Key

One source suggests this island may have been christened for an obscure, early surveyor by the same name.[23] It is far more likely, however, that the key was named by John Gerard William De Brahm, who conducted a survey of the area in 1772 for Britain.[24] De Brahm bestowed honor on his benefactors by naming features for them. An educated guess would have it that the island was named for Sir Gilbert Elliott (1722-1777) who was a Commissioner in the British Treasury and later an Member of Parliament. Previous to De Brahm, Romans called it Ledbury after the 1769 wreck of a ship by that name.[25]

Featherbed Bank
Sea plumes, particularly those of the genus *Pseudopterogorgia*, are tall, feather-like soft corals that occur commonly in the coastal waters of South Florida.[26] While no other evidence has been uncovered to explain this particular place name, it is plausible the moniker originated due to a profusion of such sea plumes in the area.

Fender Point
While earlier maps have, at one time, identified this same locale as "Finders Point", no explanation currently exists to unravel the mystery of this moniker.

Fowey Rocks
In reference to Fowey Rocks, Brookfield and Griswold note that "Many a ledge on the Florida Reef bears the name of a ship wrecked or stranded there long ago."[27] In this instance, these rocks are named for the H.M.S. *Fowey*, a British war vessel that sank here. Christened after the English town in Cornwall, the frigate struck these rocks and sank on Triumph Reef in 1748.[28] The photo shows Fowey lighthouse in 1890. *See also Soldier Key.*

Gold Key
Surveyor George Gould labored here on behalf of the Admiralty and the name of this island may be a corruption of his own name.[29] However, many of the Florida keys have also been reputed to hold vast quantities of plundered booty and it is up to the imagination of the reader as to which account is more salient.

Hawk Channel
British surveyor John Gerard William De Brahm (1717-1796) is credited with christening this channel as such in 1772. Sadly, it remains unclear who or what he was commemorating in the process.[30] Still, it seems possible to make several well-educated guesses regarding its origins.

One possible explanation would be the presence of fish hawks along the waterway. Commonly referred to today as ospreys, *Pandion haliaetus*, these raptors are often found patrolling coastal waters in search of fish swimming in the shallows.

While this may seem plausible at first, it is interesting to note that De Brahm actually christens the waterway as "Hawke Channel". Given De Brahm's particular spelling, an alternate explanation seems more probable. In *The Atlantic Pilot*, the surveyor's account of southeast Florida, De Brahm acknowledges a number of his supporters and financiers by naming islands and geographic features in their honor. To the modern reader, however, many of the names are cryptic and have retained little significance. Such is likely the fate of whomever may have been the original namesake for this feature.

However, it has been noted that one of the primary purposes of De Brahm's survey appears to be the promotion of Hawk Channel as a safe and strategic artery for commerce. Given its importance to De Brahm, one might speculate that whoever is honored with this moniker (possibly Edward Hawke, First Lord of the Admiralty) was held in high regard.[31]

Hurricane Creek

Numerous accounts exist of coastal South Florida settlers riding out tropical cyclones in boats wedged between the protective enclosures formed by mangroves.[32] Vessels moored in such locations would be spared the harshest winds of the storm and act as breaks for the surge of sea water that accompanied them. While no doubt a harrowing experience, the practice probably afforded residents far better protection than could be guaranteed in the poorly-built homes of the time. It is probable that this narrow mangrove channel earned its moniker from just such use.

While this practice may simply seem to be a custom of old, it has been noted that a great many boat owners among the Florida Keys and Ten Thousand Islands still use this method today as a means of protecting their craft during even the most intense hurricanes![33]

Jones Lagoon

Israel Lafayette Jones, otherwise known as "Parson Jones", hailed from Raleigh, North Carolina. Between 1897 and 1899, this resourceful black man purchased Porgy Key for $300.[34] He proceeded to homestead the island with his wife Mozelle and two sons, Arthur and Lancelot (named for the famed heroes of Camelot).

Here the family prospered growing limes, grapefruit and pineapples. Jones was also a respected bonefishing guide. He died in 1932, followed only a few years later by the death of Mozelle.[35] After a life of military service, Arthur died in 1966. All told, the family owned more than 250 acres spanning over three islands situated around a shallow water lagoon.[36]

Lancelot Jones remained as a property owner on Porgy Key, moving eventually to a secluded shack among the mangroves of Totten Key.[37] In the tradition of his father, he continued to guide fishermen in search of bonefish around the shallow waters of the islands. During the early 1970s, Lancelot sold the whole of his property to the National Park Service for inclusion in Biscayne National Monument.

For all that the family did for the area, it is fitting that that this lagoon still bears the Jones name to this day.

Legare Anchorage

In a letter to his Superintendent in 1852, Lieutenant Commander John Rodgers of the U.S. Steamer *Legare* writes of the discovery of a harbor of refuge near Triumph Reef. In his letter, Rodgers says of the harbor that it is "easy of access, near the Gulf Stream, and may be used without a pilot, but it needs buoys to define its place." Today, markers do, in fact, delineate portions of the anchorage.

Rodgers felt comfortable naming the discovery for his ship, writing "The reefs are called after the vessels which are wrecked on them; there seems a propriety in calling harbors after the vessels which discover them."[38]

Lewis Cut
Currently, no evidence has been uncovered to explain the origins of this particular place name, although it could commemorate an old pioneering family.[39]

Long Reef
True to its name, this reef comprises one of the longest contiguous tracts of coral in the park – over two full miles!

Lugano Wreck
The British steamer *Lugano* went aground on Long Reef during foul weather in 1913. While her 116 passengers were spared and $1 million cargo salvaged, the vessel would not be so lucky. High winds and rough seas continued to batter the vessel for over a month before efforts were abandoned and the ship regarded as a total loss. Today, only the hull remains, resting peaceably in only twenty-five feet of water.[40]

Mandalay Wreck
In the early morning hours of New Years Day in 1966, a steel schooner by the name of the *Mandalay* ran hard aground roughly 20 miles southeast of Miami. The 128-foot windjammer hosted twenty-three vacationers and twelve crew men on a ten-day Bahamian cruise. In the midst of 10-foot waves and hefty rains, victims were plucked from rafts by Coast Guard helicopters and flown to the Homestead Air Force Base nearby. Others were whisked by patrol boat to the Coast Guard base at Miami Beach.[41]

With all passengers safe, the vessel's owner, Mike Burke, still hoped to save the *Mandalay*. "It looks promising to save her, " Burke was reported to say, "but we'll probably have to wait for high tide." But such would not be the case for the vessel that Burke once called "the red carpet ship of the windjammer reef." Looters stripped the vessel of all her valuables before salvage tugs could aid her. To add insult to injury, during the course of trying to free her, the hull ruptured and filled with water, sending the ship to the grasp of the reef. The *Mandalay* remains there today, one of the prettiest dives in the park, lying in only ten feet of water at high tide.[42]

Mangrove Point, Mangrove Key
"Mangrove" is a generic word used to describe a number of trees that grow in or near saltwater. The term itself does not signify a particular botanical relation. Rather, in South Florida, our mangroves consist of four species, representing four different genera and three families.[43]

Many visitors to South Florida are surprised at the relative dearth of accessible beaches in the area. Successful tourism marketing has created the illusion that pure, white-sand beaches await you on every stretch of shoreline you encounter. In truth, the vast majority of our coast is dominated by impenetrable forests of mangroves that do not allow easy access to the ocean. And behind the few areas where sand does deposit to form a beach, there usually exists a band of mangroves preventing its enjoyment.

The ecological value of mangroves has been recognized throughout world. By rooting in the salt water of the tropics, these amazing trees defy our most basic preconceptions about plants. In doing so, they also form a tangle of vegetation in the warm shallows, which serve as important nursery grounds for a number of commercially and recreationally important species. For terrestrial life along the coast, mangroves also represent the first line of defense against the devastating winds of tropical storms. In light of these contributions, mangroves have been granted strict protection in the state of Florida.

South Florida boasts the largest stand of protected mangrove forest in the Western Hemisphere. Given our growing conditions, one can surmise that at one time or another every inch of coastline has grown thick with these trees. Thus, it is curious why this particular spit of land, though draped with mangroves, should be singled out for this distinction.

The tiny key lies just offshore of Mangrove Point.

Margot Fish Shoal
No documentation has been uncovered to explain the origins of this particular place name.

Midnight Pass
Given the historic profusion of illicit activities around the Florida coast, one can dream up many a fanciful explanation for this particular moniker. Though thoughts of pirates, rum runners, and drug smugglers go far to fuel the imagination, the true origins of this place name remain a mystery.

Old Rhodes Key
It has been speculated that this key may have been named after the isle of Rhodes in the Mediterranean, or for the Rose Island Rocks in the Bahamas. This does only represent a "best educated guess", as no better explanation currently exists.[44]

Ott Point
The origin of this particular moniker is unknown, but what follows represents the best guess to date. To decipher the cryptic puzzle of this name, it is necessary to examine several maps of Biscayne Bay. In most maps, the name "Elliott Key" is written roughly in the same place. Consequently, the "ott" in this label lands conspicuously in the same location on each – roughly around a small jut of land on the west side of the island![45]

Pacific Reef
Currently, it is unclear how this reef earned its current moniker.

Pelican Bank
This area of shallows is no doubt named for the common appearance of the brown pelican, *Pelecanus occidentalis* – one of the many birds that can be found resting on this shoal during low tides. *See also Pelican Keys in Everglades National Park.*

Petrel Point
Storm Petrels are oceanic birds that are rarely seen around land. They are truly pelagic and are known to come ashore only to breed.[46] Both the Wilson's Storm-Petrel, *Oceanites oceanicus*, and the Leach's Storm-Petrel, *Oceanodroma leucorhoa* have been sighted in South Florida on rare occasions.[47] But given the scarcity of these birds in the area, it is highly unlikely that either species gave rise to this particular place name.

It is far more likely that this spit of land was named for the *Petrel*, a schooner employed during the coastal surveys of the 1850s. Under the command of Lieutenant Joseph Totten, the ship and her crew were instrumental in performing topographic explorations of the area, and used such points for triangulation.[48] Given the party's known proclivity for naming geographic features for ships, contemporaries and superiors, it is not hard to imagine the origins of this moniker.

Point Adelle
Sadly, it appears no information persists to explain why this small spit of land bears this attractive name.

Porgy Key
Sub-Assistant I. H. Adams of the United States Coastal Survey named this island "Porgee Key" in 1854, though he offered no explanation for the moniker.[49] Still, it is likely that the island is named for the sheepshead, a member of a family of fish often referred to as "porgies" and an abundant resident in these waters.[50]

Ragged Keys
The ragged keys may have derived their names from the fact that they appeared for many years, and even today, as scarcely little more than shoals showing above the surface of the water.[51]

Reid Key
Sub-Assistant I. H. Adams of the United States Coastal Survey named this island in 1854, though he offered no explanation for the moniker.[52]

Rocky Reef

No evidence is currently available to explain the origins of this particular moniker. It appears to be no rockier than other reefs.

Rubicon Keys

This island was given its name by the United States Coastal Survey in 1854.[53] It has been theorized that the moniker honors a famous historical event.[54] Playing upon the name of Caesar's Creek, they no doubt christened this island after the Rubicon River of northern Italy. In 49 B.C., Julius Caesar would come to cross this small outlet to the Adriatic Sea, sparking civil war. His actions would eventually bring about the famed Roman Empire and earn him the title of emperor.[55]

Safety Valve

Commodore Ralph Middleton Munroe (1851-1933) is credited with naming this naturally engineered feature in Biscayne Bay. Following years of observation, he concluded that the span of water between Key Biscayne and the Ragged Keys served as an outlet for excessive storm water, preventing flooding in the north end of the bay. The name was approved by the United States Geographic Board in 1927.[56]

Sands Key, Sands Cut

During his visit here during the 1760's, Bernard Romans, a surveyor for the British government, visited what is now known as Sands Key. Upon what appears to be little more than a flat patch of sand he found two shell mounds that were most probably the work of island dwellers long ago. He reported that the resulting pair of small hills inspired the Spaniards before him to refer to this island as "Las Tetas".[57]

In his 1775 account, Romans calls this small island, "Saunder's Key", possibly to honor Sir Charles Saunders who was First Lord of the Admiralty from 1766 to 1771. It is plausible that over time, that name has been corrupted to its current form.

The cut is a natural channel that runs between Sands Key to the north and Elliott Key to the south.

Sandwich Cove

William Gerard de Brahm surveyed the entire east coast of Florida following the English acquisition of Florida in the mid-1700s. During this work, de Brahm honored a number of prominent Englishmen of his time. One of his maps clearly shows the whole of Biscayne Bay as "Sandwich Gulf", presumably named for the 4th Earl of Sandwich (1718-1792), First Lord of the Admiralty from 1771 to 1782. What is now known as Sandwich Cove may be all that remains to remind us of this obscure, early moniker.[58]

Schooner Wreck

This particular location is named for a large ballast pile that can be found here. While no corroborating evidence has been found, it is presumed to be the remains of a schooner that wrecked here.[59]

Sea Grape Point

The sea grape, *Coccoloba uvifera*, is a common tree along the South Florida coastline. This handsome species often sports a broad, shady crown composed of numerous large, circular leaves. As the name implies, its pulpy fruits are borne in bunches and are highly attractive to wildlife. The fruits are also collected to make tasty jams and jellies.

The sea grape can be found around coastal hammocks and beach strands throughout the southern peninsula.[60] Why this designation has been bestowed upon this particular piece of land is unclear at this time.

Soldier Key

Although this place name dates back to at least 1775 and is of unknown origin, it nonetheless seems appropriate. In 1878, the Federal government built a new lighthouse on Fowey Rocks as a replacement for the light on Key Biscayne.[61] Construction of the light was undertaken by the U.S. military, who erected a series of facilities on this nearby key to house the workers. *See also Fowey Rocks.*

In 1898, Hugh Willoughby recorded of his visit to the area, "The nearest land to the [Fowey] 'Light' is a little island called Soldier Key, which was used by the constructing engineers to work upon and for a supply station. The old buildings are still to be seen, though they have never had any attention or care since."[62] To this day, foundations of old structures can been found upon the tiny island.

Star Reef

Richard Curry, science coordinator for Biscayne National Park, notes that this popular dive spot derives its current moniker from the prominence of star coral on the reef.[63]

Several species of star coral occur along the Florida Coast. Two of the more conspicuous among them are boulder star coral, *Montastraea annularis*, and the great star coral, *Montastrea cavernosa*.[64] Both occur in relatively shallow waters and form prominent, picturesque colonies that attract a rich diversity of marine life.

Stiltsville

"Crawfish Eddie" was an affable type who sold bait and chowder in the Biscayne Channel off of Cape Florida. Well regarded as a great spinner of yarns, locals would gather at his offshore locale to slurp down chowder and listen to his many tales.

Owing largely to the presence of "Crawfish Charlie", as he was also known, the waters around the Biscayne Channel became a favorite haunt. Nearby residents began constructing weekend retreats upon the hulls of several beached vessels in the area.

As the 1950s went on, certain movers and shakers in Miami began building homes on stilts around the channel, by pounding rods into the hard bottom of the shallow waters of Biscayne Bay.[65] Despite the damage inflicted by numerous tropical storms, the stilted structures remain to this day, and have given rise to the area's current moniker.

Swan Key

This appellation is one of many in the park that remain a mystery to this day.

The Drop
This geologic feature derives its name for the fact that the area slopes from a depth of 40 feet to roughly 80 feet. It has been suggested that this quick change in depth seems to indicate where the former shoreline of southeast Florida may have existed at one time. [66]

Totten Key
In recounting the many prominent individuals that have spent time in the area that would one day become Biscayne National Park, Carter Burrus writes of the visit of Colonel Robert E. Lee. The famed Civil War figure was encouraged to survey the area to report on the condition of local military installations. Burrus suggests that it can be assumed that Totten Key was named by Lee himself in honor of his commanding officer at the time, Joseph Gilbert Totten, who would later become Brigadier General of the Army Corps of Engineers in 1863. [67]

An 1854 report on the status of U.S. coastal survey efforts, however, reveals a different story. As it turns out, the islands stretching between Caesar's Creek and Old Rhodes Key were christened in the same year by Officer I. H. Adams of the coastal survey. During this project, Adams served as Sub-Assistant to Lieutenant James Totten of the United States Army. [68] In his correspondence, Adams does not specify for whom the keys are named, but it is probable that the designation was meant to honor his commanding officer.

Still, one more wrinkle adds a bit of uncertainty to this explanation. As it turns out, a second Lieutenant by the name of Joseph Swift Totten, served as an officer in the survey of the South Florida coast. Well regarded among his peers and admired for his diligence of work, he would meet an untimely death during the same year due to an unspecified illness. [69] It is possible, therefore, that this island had been so christened to honor his memory.

Triumph Reef
Though a bit deeper than most, this reef remains one of the prettiest dives in the park. Unfortunately, no evidence has been uncovered to reveal the origins of this intriguing moniker.

Turkey Point

While not within the confines of the park, this facility bears a tremendous influence on the area. Few national parks boast nuclear power plants as neighbors. Although the massive structure is clearly the dominating feature of this location today, it was not always the case.

Carter Burrus writes, "Turkey Point was an 18,000-acre wilderness area of mud flats and mangrove thicket edged by Biscayne Bay. It included a neck of land with two blunted points, somewhat the shape of a turkey's neck, jutting into the bay."[70]

While this may explain the origins of the moniker, it is more probable to believe that a common coastal species is the true namesake. The ubiquitous Anhinga, known locally as the "water turkey", may have congregated and/or nested here at one time.

University Dock

This structure was first built by the University Yacht Club prior to the establishment of Biscayne National Monument, though the National Park Service did rebuild the dock in the 1980s.[71]

REFERENCES

[1] Bloodworth, Bertha Ernestine. *Florida Place-Names*. University of Florida. August 1959. Pg. 118.

[2] Fontaneda, Hernando. d'Escalante *Memoire of Do. d'Esdalante Fontaneda Respecting Florida*. 1854. Trans. B. Smith. Washington, D.C. Reprinted Coral Gables: Univ.Miami Press. 1944.

[3] Goggin, John M. "Archaeological Investigations of the Upper Florida Keys". *Tequesta: The Journal of the Historical Association of Southern Florida*. 1944. No. 4.

[4] University of Miami. *A Tribute to Dante B. Fascell*. January 22, 1999.

[5] Bache, Alexander Dallas. *Report of the Superintendent of the Coast Survey*. National Oceanographic and Atmospheric Administration. 1852-1856.

[6] Berg, Daniel & Denise. *Florida Shipwrecks*. Aqua Explorers Inc. East Rockaway, NY. 1991.

[7] Berg, Daniel & Denise. *Florida Shipwrecks*. Aqua Explorers Inc. East Rockaway, NY. 1991. Pg. 7.

[8] Curry, Richard. *Personal Commentary*. December 7, 2004.

[9] Brookfield, Charles Mann. Interview by Love Dean. Early 1982. Islamorada Branch, Monroe Public Library. Later printed as an article for *Florida Keys Magazine*, First Quarter 1982.

[10] Henry, Joseph. 1872. "Eulogy on Prof. Alexander Dallas Bache." In: *Annual Report of the Board of Regents of the Smithsonian Institution, Showing the Operations, Expenditures, and Condition of the Institution for the Year 1870*. 42nd Congress, 1st Session, House of Representatives, Ex. Doc. No. 20. Government Printing Office, Washington, D.C. Pgs. 91-108.

[11] Curry, Richard. *Personal Commentary*. December 7, 2004.

[12] Helmers, Terry. *Personal Commentary*. 2006.

[13] Burrus, E. Carter, Jr. *A History of the Islands and Waters of Biscayne National Park*. Doctoral Dissertation. Univeristy of Miami. Miami, FL. 1984. Pg. 74.

[14] Derr, Mark. *Some Kind of Paradise. A Chronicle of Man and the Land In Florida*. University Press of Florida. Gainesville, FL. 1998. Pgs. 276-277.

[15] Singer, Steven D. *Shipwrecks of Florida: A Comprehensive Listing*. Pineapple Press. Sarasota, FL. 1998. Pg. 117.

[16] McCarthy, Kevin M. & William L Trotter. *Twenty Florida Pirates*. Pineapple Press. Sarasota, FL 1994. Pgs. 39-41.

[17] Maynel, Anthony D. *Chart of the Gulf of Florida and Providence N.W. Channel*. 1820 & 1821.

[18] *Map of Miami-Dade County, 1890*. Geo F. Cram, Engraver & Publisher, Chicago, IL.

[19] Bloodworth, Bertha Ernestine. *Florida Place-Names*. University of Florida. August 1959. Pg. 200

[20] Bache, Alexander Dallas. *Report of the Superintendent of the Coast Survey*. National Oceanographic and Atmospheric Administration. 1852-1856.

[21] Human, Paul. *Reef Coral Identification*. New World Publications. Jacksonville, FL. 1993. Pg. 93.

[22] NOAA Fisheries. *General Fact Sheet Atlantic Acropora Corals*. 2006.

[23] 16] Brookfield, Charles Mann. Interview by Love Dean. Early 1982. Islamorada Branch, Monroe Public Library. Later printed as an article for *Florida Keys Magazine*, First Quarter 1982.

[24] De Brahm, John Gerard William. *The Atlantic Pilot*. T. Spilsbury. London, England. 1772. Reprint 1974. Pg. 4.

[25] Romans, Bernard. *A Concise Natural History of East and West Florida*. 1775. Reprinted by Pelican Publishing Company. New Orleans, LA. 1998. Pg. 248.

[26] Human, Paul. *Reef Coral Identification*. New World Publications. Jacksonville, FL. 1993.

[27] Brookfield, Charles M. & Oliver Griswold. *They All Called it Tropical*. Historical Association of Southern Florida. Miami, FL. 1949. Pg. 18.

[28] Lenihan, Daniel. *Submerged: Adventures of America's Most Elite Underwater Archeology Team*. Newmarket Press. New York, NY. 2002.

[29] Burrus, E. Carter, Jr. *A History of the Islands and Waters of Biscayne National Park*. Doctoral Dissertation. Univeristy of Miami. Miami, FL. 1984. Pg. 30.

[30] De Brahm, John Gerard William. *The Atlantic Pilot*. T. Spilsbury. London, England. 1772. Reprint 1974. Pg. 41.

[31] De Brahm, John Gerard William. *The Atlantic Pilot*. T. Spilsbury. London, England. 1772. Reprint 1974. Pg. 53.

[32] Tebeau, Charlton W. *Man in the Everglades*. University of Miami Press. Miami, FL. 1968. Pg. 110.

[33] Sohn, Amara. *NBC6 Evening News*. August 29. Miami, FL. 2006.

[34] O'Connell, Kim A. "The Keepers of the Keys". *National Parks*. May/June 2003. Pgs. 30-31.

[35] Burrus, E. Carter, Jr. *A History of the Islands and Waters of Biscayne National Park*. Doctoral Dissertation. Univeristy of Miami. Miami, FL. 1984. Pg. 75.

[36] O'Connell, Kim A. "The Keepers of the Keys". *National Parks*. May/June 2003. Pg. 31

[37] Wilker, Debbie. "Islandia: Last Man in a City of the Sea is Busy, Content". *The Miami News*. November 25, 1985.

[38] Rodgers, John. *Report of The Superintendent of the Coast Survey, Showing The Progress of the Survey During the Year 1852*. 1853. United States Coast Survey.

[39] Wilkinson, Jerry. Historical Preservation Society of the Upper Keys. www.keyshistory.org.

[40] National Park Service. *Maritime Heritage Trail Website*. 2006. www.nps.gov/bisc.

[41] Archbold, Rich & Cele Ferner. "Ends 'Leisurely Adventure Trip'". *The Miami Herald*. January 1, 1966.

[42] Helmers, Terry. *Mandalay*. Biscayne National Park Archives. n/d.

[43] Wunderlin, Richard P. *Guide to the Vascular Plants of Florida*. University Press of Florida. Gainesville, FL. 1998.

[44] Burrus, E. Carter, Jr. *A History of the Islands and Waters of Biscayne National Park*. Doctoral Dissertation. Univeristy of Miami. Miami, FL. 1984. Pg. 28.

[45] Lazendorf, Brenda. *Personal Commentary*. December 7, 2004.

[46] Sibley, David Allen. *The Sibley Guide to Birds*. Alfred A. Knopf. New York. 2000. Pg. 41-43.

[47] National Park Service. *Bird Checklist of Everglades National Park*. 2005.

[48] Bache, Alexander Dallas. *Report of the Superintendent of the Coast Survey*. National Oceanographic and Atmospheric Administration. 1852-1856.

[49] Bache, Alexander Dallas. *Report of the Superintendent of the Coast Survey*. National Oceanographic and Atmospheric Administration. 1852-1856.

[50] Cochran, Gary. *Florida's Fabulous Fishes*. World Publications. Tampa, FL. 2003. Pg. 87.

[51] Oppel, Frank & Tony Meisel. *Tales of Old Florida*. Book Sales, Inc. Secaucus, NJ. 1987. Pg. 22.

[52] Bache, Alexander Dallas. *Report of the Superintendent of the Coast Survey*. National Oceanographic and Atmospheric Administration. National Oceanographic and Atmospheric Administration. 1852-1856.

[53] Bache, Alexander Dallas. *Report of the Superintendent of the Coast Survey*. National Oceanographic and Atmospheric Administration. 1852-1856.

[54] Brookfield, Charles Mann. Interview by Love Dean. Early 1982. Islamorada Branch, Monroe Public Library. Later printed as an article for *Florida Keys Magazine*, First Quarter 1982.

[55] Suetonius, transl. Alexander Thompson. *The Lives of the Twelve Caesars*. G. Bell & Sons, 1893.

[56] "Islet's New Name is Safety Valve". *Miami Herald*. May 8, 1927. Page 35.

[57] Romans, Bernard. *A Concise Natural History of East and West Florida*. 1775. Reprinted by Pelican Publishing Company. New Orleans, LA. 1998. Pg. 247.

[58] Burrus, E. Carter, Jr. *A History of the Islands and Waters of Biscayne National Park*. Doctoral Dissertation. Univeristy of Miami. Miami, FL. 1984. Pg. 27.

[59] Curry, Richard. *Personal Commentary*. December 7, 2004.

[60] Wunderlin, Richard P. *Guide to the Vascular Plants of Florida*. University Press of Florida. Gainesville, FL. 1998. Pg. 270.

[61] Oppel, Frank & Tony Meisel. *Tales of Old Florida*. Book Sales, Inc. Secaucus, NJ. 1987. Pg. 22.

[62] Willoughby, Hugh L. *Across the Everglades*. Florida Classics Library. Port Selerno, FL. 1898. Pg. 67.

[63] Curry, Richard. *Personal Commentary*. December 7, 2004.

[64] Human, Paul. *Reef Coral Identification*. New World Publications. Jacksonville, FL. 1993.

[65] Dr. Paul George. *Personal Commentary*. April 3, 2005.

[66] Curry, Richard. *Personal Commentary*. December 7, 2004.

[67] Burrus, E. Carter, Jr. *A History of the Islands and Waters of Biscayne National Park*. Doctoral Dissertation. Univeristy of Miami. Miami, FL. 1984. Pg. 40.

[68] Bache, Alexander Dallas. *Report of the Superintendent of the Coast Survey*. National Oceanographic and Atmospheric Administration. 1852-1856.

[69] Bache, Alexander Dallas. Administration. *Report of the Superintendent of the Coast Survey*. National Oceanographic and Atmospheric 1852-1856

[70] Burrus, E. Carter, Jr. *A History of the Islands and Waters of Biscayne National Park*. Doctoral Dissertation. Univeristy of Miami. Miami, FL. 1984. Pg. 100.

[71] Curry, Richard. *Personal Commentary*. December 7, 2004.

Chapter 3

DRY TORTUGAS NATIONAL PARK

Dry Tortugas remains one of our most isolated national parks. Visitors hoping to reach this jewel must travel the length of the Florida peninsula to its terminus in Miami. From there, it is roughly 130 miles across the Overseas Highway to the last of the Florida Keys. From Key West, the Tortugas lie still 70 miles into the Gulf, accessible only by ferry or sea plane.

Visitors able to make the journey are first greeted with a view of massive Fort Jefferson. Though never having seen a shot fired in battle, the islands of the Tortugas are richly steeped in military history. Walking only a few steps among the walls of this lumbering fortification transports visitors back in time to the sagas of the Civil and Spanish-American Wars. Relegated to use as a military prison, the fort would come to house numerous confederate captives, including Doctor Samuel Mudd, who famously set the broken leg of Lincoln assassin John Wilkes Booth. Here live memories of hardship and struggle amidst yellow fever, poor rations, and palpable desolation. It is upon this stage that many soldiers, and their ships, eventually foundered.

Perched gingerly above the Gulf Stream, the Dry Tortugas have been silent witnesses to maritime history. Since the early arrival of Ponce de Leon, the islands have seen an endless cavalcade of human visitors that continues to this day. Explorers, pirates, surveyors, engineers, soldiers, prisoners, scientists, fishermen, sightseers and park rangers complete the compliment and continue to contribute to the history of these intriguing islands. You, too, have the opportunity to pen a chapter in the story.

There are only twenty-two named locations to be found on the map of Dry Tortugas National Park. Though few, these monikers hint at an island chain that once was, and yet one day may become again.

Dry Tortugas

In the year 1513, this cluster of small islands yielded important provisions for the crew of the Spanish explorer Juan Ponce de Leon. Among these were scores of sea turtles, which provided eggs and meat for the long journey ahead. It has been written that the crew were able to capture one hundred and seventy turtles along the beach.[1] Owing to the numbers in which they were present, Ponce de Leon christened them "Las Islas de Las Tortugas".

While the islands boasted many resources, fresh water was not to be found there. The word "dry" was later added to navigation charts to alert mariners to this condition.[2]

Fort Jefferson

Fort Jefferson is one of the largest nineteenth-century coastal forts in America.[3] Secretary of War Charles M. Conrad has been credited with christening the structure with its current moniker on October 8, 1850. It was named in honor of the third president of the United States, Thomas Jefferson (1743-1826).[4]

Geographic Features

Bird Key Anchorage
This area once provided safe harbor near Bird Key.

Bird Key Bank
At one point in history, the Tortugas consisted of 8 islands, including one named Bird Key. During his explorations of the area in 1832, John James Audubon reported seeing great quantities of sooty terns, *Onychoprion fuscata*, on this tiny island, which in subsequent years became prime nesting grounds also for brown noddies, *Anous stolidus*. It is probable that the island derived its current moniker from this function.

In subsequent years, the island would host a variety of other uses. Beginning in 1860, soldiers infected with smallpox were quarantined here in a small, wood-frame hospital.[5] Around the same time, a gun battery was constructed on the island, and plans were developed for the construction of a permanent fort. For reasons unknown, these plans were never brought to fruition. The island also served as a burial ground for the deceased.[6]

Following years of gradual erosion, the tiny island finally washed away under the fierce winds of the Labor Day Hurricane of 1935. It was situated in the vicinity of this bank which still bears its name.[7]

Brick Wreck
This unfortunate vessel, dating back to the 1850s, found its final resting place in the shallows of the Bird Key Anchorage.[8] This wreck lies in shallow water close to Garden Key. Most notable among the many artifacts strewn about the site is an abundance of bricks. It is unclear whether this cargo was being taken to Garden Key during the construction of Fort Jefferson or was being taken from it at a later date.[9] While it has been speculated that this ship may have been the *Scottish Chief*, it has never been positively identified and is known to this day only as the "Brick Wreck" or the "Bird Key Wreck".[10]

Brilliant Shoal

While the term "shoal" is used to denote an area of shallow water, no evidence currently exists to explain the origins of this particular place name.

Bush Key

This island was reportedly heavily vegetated prior to a hurricane that struck the area in 1870. The key all but vanished in the storm's aftermath, though it has resurrected in subsequent years.[11]

Today, the island serves as a crucial nesting ground for sooty terns (seen in this 1939 photo) and brown noddies. The birds that come to the Dry Tortugas constitute the only nesting colonies of these species in the continental United States.[12]

East Key

Some names just make sense! This key, for example, derives its name from the fact that it is the most eastern island of the Dry Tortugas[13]. So simple its *scary*!

Garden Key

While the parade grounds of Fort Jefferson did, at one time, host a small garden of tamarinds, guavas, date palms and coconut trees, the moniker "Garden Key" far predated the construction of the fort.[14]

Sadly, there is no evidence that explains the meaning behind this place name. Rather, there is some confusion as to its origins. The name does not appear on the earliest survey known of the area, and subsequently has been referred to as "Gorden" Key.[15] This will likely remain a tantalizing mystery among the islands.

Hospital Key

Formerly known as Sand Key, this island boasts little vegetation and resembles little more than a small sandbar. During the building of Fort Jefferson, the key served as the primary source of sand for construction.[16]

It has been noted that during the 1860s, the island was used for the isolation of patients with yellow fever, hence the current moniker.[17] A small ten-person hospital was maintained there, and the former presence of monument stones provided testament to this island's alternate use as a final resting place for the dead.[18] In fact, many of the 206 recorded burials in the Dry Tortugas occurred there.[19]

Iowa Rock
Though no battles would take place here, the isolated Dry Tortugas served as the backdrop for considerable military activity in early 1898. In the months preceding the outbreak of the Spanish-American War, maneuvers were practiced on the tiny islands, numerous warships anchored in the harbor, and one seaman would lose his life in a tragic accident off Sandy Key.

The list of ships anchored off Garden Key during this time reads like a map of the United States: *Massachusetts*, *Indiana*, *New York*, *Texas*, *Detroit*. The *USS Maine* departed the Tortugas on its ill-fated voyage to Cuba on January 24, 1898. Only three days later, another battleship, the *Iowa*, would run aground near Garden Key and forever give its name to the tiny shoal on which it became stranded.[20] The ship would be freed in only a day, and would begin intense service in the blockade of Cuba following the sinking of the *Maine* on February 16.

Little Africa
Most visitors to the Dry Tortugas would be understandably stumped by this particular moniker. To understand it, one must observe the reef from the vantage point of the lighthouse on Loggerhead Key. Looking out from atop the light, one cannot help but notice that the outline of the reef does bear a striking resemblance to the shape of the dark continent.[21]

Loggerhead Key, Loggerhead Reef
The largest island of the Dry Tortugas derives its name from the most common sea turtle to inhabit the area. The loggerhead, *Caretta caretta*, is the most ubiquitous of several species of sea turtles that inhabit the waters of the Dry Tortugas, and is Federally protected as a threatened species.[22]

Loggerhead Reef, which lies just southwest of this island, probably derives its name from its proximity to the Key.

Long Key
As this is far from the longest island in the Tortugas chain, it is curious why it would earn such a moniker.

Middle Ground
An entry in the Oxford English Dictionary defines "middle ground" as "a shallow place, as a bank or bar."[23] This definition certainly holds true here, as this shallow embankment lies within an area of open water between Hospital and Loggerhead Keys.

Middle Key
This island is situated roughly equidistant between East Key and Hospital Key. This positioning no doubt gave rise to its current name.

Northkey Harbor
A visit to the Dry Tortugas during the late 1880s would have revealed eleven islands in existence rather than the seven you find today. The cyclic forces of nature continue to wash away old islands from one location only to build up again somewhere else.

One of the area's former islands was North Key, which was located roughly were its namesake harbor is shown today. Perhaps a hundred years in the future, the sands of this mystery island will build up once again to form a "New North Key"! [24]

Pulaski Shoal
It is probable that this embankment is named for Count Casimir Pulaski (1746-1779). A Polish-born soldier, Pulaski would famously lead the American cavalry against the British during the Siege of Savannah in 1779, during which he died of gunshot wounds. While he is honored most notably as the namesake of Fort Pulaski in Georgia, no evidence exists as to why this area might also commemorate his memory.

Texas Rock
Named for the battleship *USS Texas* which ran aground here immediately preceding the Spanish-American War. *See also Iowa Rock.*

White Shoal
No evidence exists to explain the origins of this moniker.

Windjammer Wreck
In 1901, the windjammer *Avanti* began transporting timber from Pensacola to the Caribbean. The iron-hulled, ship-rigged sailing vessel continued to meet the demands of the growing timber industry until January 21, 1907, [25] when she sank near Loggerhead Key under unknown circumstances.[26]

Owing perhaps to iron's resistance to corrosion, the *Avanti* remains well-preserved, beckoning a wide variety of sea life to colonize along its length. The "Windjammer Wreck" continues to be one of the more popular sites for snorkelers and divers.[27]

Dry Tortugas National Park

REFERENCES

[1] Gifford, John C. *The Rehabilitation of the Florida Keys*. Lewis Adams' Colonial Press. 1934. Pgs. 65-67.

[2] Landrum, L. Wayne. *Fort Jefferson and the Dry Tortugas National Park*. Wayne Landrum. Big Pine Key, FL. 2003. Pg. 5.

[3] National Park Service. *Dry Tortugas Official Map and Guide*. 2004.

[4] Bearss, Edwin C. *Historic Structure Report Historical Data Section Fort Jefferson: 1846-1898*. National Park Service. July 1983. Pg. 87.

[5] Bearss, Edwin C. *Historic Structure Report Historical Data Section Fort Jefferson: 1846-1898*. National Park Service. July 1983.

[6] Ryan, Mike T, *Personal Commentary*, August 29, 2006.

[7] Tebeau, Charlton W. *Man in the Everglades*. University of Miami Press. Miami, FL. 1968. Pgs. 33-34.

[8] Landrum, L. Wayne. *Fort Jefferson and the Dry Tortugas National Park*. Wayne Landrum. Big Pine Key, FL. 2003. Pg. 45.

[9] Barnette, Michael C. *Shipwrecks of the Sunshine State*. Association of Underwater Explorers. 2003. Pg. 165.

[10] Shull, Carol D. *Florida Shipwrecks: 300 Years of Maritime History*. National Park Service. Washington, D.C. 2005.

[11] Tebeau, Charlton W. *Man in the Everglades*. University of Miami Press. Miami, FL. 1968. Pg. 34.

[12] Sibley, David Allen. *The Sibley Field Guide to Birds of Eastern North America*. Alfred A. Knopf, New York, NY. 2003. Pgs. 196-197.

[13] Landrum, L. Wayne. *Fort Jefferson and the Dry Tortugas National Park*. Wayne Landrum. Big Pine Key, FL. 2003. Pg. 9.

[14] Murphy, Larry E. Editor. *Dry Tortugas National Park Submerged Cultural Resources Assessment*. National Park Service. Santa Fe, New Mexico. 1993. Pg. 137.

[15] Murphy, Larry E. Editor. *Dry Tortugas National Park Submerged Cultural Resources Assessment*. National Park Service. Santa Fe, New Mexico. 1993. Pg. 225.

[16] Murphy, Larry E. Editor. *Dry Tortugas National Park Submerged Cultural Resources Assessment*. National Park Service. Santa Fe, New Mexico. 1993. Pg. 239.

[17] Tebeau, Charlton W. *Man in the Everglades*. University of Miami Press. Miami, FL. 1968. Pg 34.

[18] Murphy, Larry E. Editor. *Dry Tortugas National Park Submerged Cultural Resources Assessment*. National Park Service. Santa Fe, New Mexico. 1993. Pg. 239.

[19] Ryan, Mike T., *Personal Commentary*, August 29, 2006.

[20] Ryan, Mike T., *Personal Commentary*, 2005.

[21] www.sherpaguides.com

[22] Carmichael, Pete & Winston Williams. *Florida's Fabulous Reptiles and Amphibians*. World Publications. 1991. Pg. 116.

[23] McMullen, E. Wallace, Jr. *English Topographic Terms in Florida 1563-1874*. University of Florida Press. Gainesville, FL. 1953. Pg. 151.

[24] Landrum, L. Wayne. *Fort Jefferson and the Dry Tortugas National Park*. Wayne Landrum. Big Pine Key, FL. 2003. Pgs. 6-8.

[25] Murphy, Larry E. Editor. *Dry Tortugas National Park Submerged Cultural Resources Assessment*. National Park Service. Santa Fe, New Mexico. 1993. Pg. 203.

[26] Shull, Carol D. *Florida Shipwrecks: 300 Years of Maritime History*. National Park Service. Washington, D.C. 2005.

[27] Landrum, L. Wayne. *Fort Jefferson and the Dry Tortugas National Park*. Wayne Landrum. Big Pine Key, FL. 2003. Pg. 45.

Chapter 4

EVERGLADES NATIONAL PARK

The author must now be quick to point out a particular favor toward this chapter. While it has proven to be the most challenging by far, the quest to understand the colorful history of this area has been most rewarding. The nomenclature of this national park commemorates the many diverse cultures that have sought the bounty of the Everglades over hundreds of years.

A quick scan of the roughly 293 names currently shown on visitor maps reveals diverse linguistic influence from the past. Names originating from several distinct Indian cultures remind us of an often-forgotten history. Similarly, the influence of the Spanish and English is conspicuous here. While some of their terms have been corrupted over the years, they hearken back to a time of discovery and colonialism. Flavors from France help complete the story of European life in South Florida, while words of African origin provide ambience from a distant continent.

Presently, South Florida enjoys great fame for its unique fusion of diverse peoples. In this light, it is interesting to note that long before these waves of recent emigration, the wilds of the Everglades attracted settlers from around the globe. Owing perhaps to its geography and climate, it would appear that South Florida was destined to host a varied populace.

Significance aside, many of the place names in Everglades National Park are simply intriguing. Names like Graveyard Creek and Snake Bight contribute to the air of dark mystery that permeates the area. Places like Flamingo and Manatee Key bring thoughts of some of our rarest denizens. And one can only smirk at contemplating the origins of names like Dildo Key or First National Bank.

The names of Everglades National Park convey many things at once: darkness, struggle, simplicity, levity, mystery, perseverance and survival. They are a standing memorial to the experiences of those who came before.

Everglades
There is some debate regarding the origins of the name "Everglades", though the true story may never be known. The term was first used on an 1823 map and, despite variations in spelling, the area has been known as such ever since.

Today it is widely accepted that, at the time of Florida's acquisition from Spain in 1819, the term "glade" was common in the vernacular of American English. It referred to any open meadow or field of grass, usually found within a forest.[1] By contrast, in South Florida could be found a seemingly endless expanse of grass punctuated by compact islands of dense trees – hence the designation of the "Everglades".

STRUCTURES & FACILITIES

The main entrance to the park is south of Homestead but there are facilities at Shark Valley on US-41, Chekika (SW 168th Street) and at the Gulf Coast Visitor Center in Everglades City. The National Park Service also maintains boating access at Flamingo and Blackwater Sound.

Bill Robertson Building

For the better part of his career, Dr. William Beckwith Robertson, Jr. served as the senior biologist of Everglades National Park. Robertson began his employment in 1951 as a seasonal fire control aide.[2] Over the next 50 years, he would come to publish a litany of studies on the flora and fauna of the area, rapidly becoming the foremost authority on the unique Everglades landscape. In time, his systematic methodology would come to influence park science far into the future.[3]

Affectionately known as "Dr. Bill", Robertson published studies on raptor and wading bird ecology, seabird populations and pineland biology. His meticulous research often played an integral role in the management of park resources. His pioneering investigations into the effects of fire on the South Florida habitats helped give rise to the park's current fire management program.

Shortly after his passing in 2000, his name was bestowed upon the building that serves as the headquarters for the park's fire management program.

Dan Beard Research Center

Serving as an agent of the United States Fish and Wildlife Service, Daniel Beard was commissioned in 1946 to protect the future lands of Everglades National Park. Along with five deputies, Beard was given the authority to arrest anyone who flouted state game laws. After the park was formally dedicated in 1947, Beard (right in photo) was named the first superintendent[4].

Ernest Coe Visitor Center

This facility serves as the main contact station for the park, and is named for the "Father of the Everglades", Ernest Francis Coe (right in photo at the official opening of park in Everglades City in 1947). A landscape architect from Connecticut, he moved with his wife to Miami in 1925. A lover of the outdoors, Coe came to enjoy frequent expeditions into the remote Everglades. He harbored a growing fascination with the mysterious landscape and the many marvels he found there.

Large-scale attempts by developers to draw profit from the Everglades and tame the wilderness eventually led Coe to a new obsession – preservation. Prompted by devastating consequences at the hands of man, Coe was among the first of his peers to envision the Everglades as a protected national park.[5] To further his ambitious plan, he organized the Tropical Everglades National Park Association in 1928. Flanked by like-minded preservationists, Coe undertook a tireless campaign of letter-writing, meetings and lecturing. In time, his boundless enthusiasm would be rewarded. Following his appearances testifying before members of Congress, legislation authorizing the new park was passed on May 30, 1934[6] but it took until 1947 for the land to be acquired and the park to be officially opened.

Flamingo Visitor Center

Situated in the former fishing village of Flamingo, this visitor center serves as a major gateway to the coastal waters of Florida Bay and the Cape Sable area. Earlier visitors to this area may be surprised to find significant change in the aftermath of hurricanes Katrina and Wilma in 2005. *See also Flamingo.*

Gulf Coast Visitor Center

Located at the extreme western border of the park boundaries in Everglades City, this appropriately named facility serves as a visitor center and gateway to the Ten Thousand Islands.

Ingraham Highway

The Model Land Company was formed by railroad tycoon Henry Flagler in 1896 to manage his burgeoning holdings in the Sunshine State. James Edmundson Ingraham, former president of the South Florida Railroad Company, was selected to head this endeavor. Prior to his appointment, Ingraham had conducted a survey into the Everglades to assess the feasibility of extending a railway into the country. Ingraham insisted that an approach from the east coast was most favorable.[7]

The Model Land Company soon acquired an impressive amount of real estate along the Eastern coast, including a whopping 210,000 acres in the Cape Sable area. Of particular interest were the company's holdings in the vicinity of Paradise Key. A large hammock in the area was particularly well known for its botanical wonders and plentiful wildlife.

In 1910, Ingraham informed Ms. Kirk Munroe, then chairman of the Florida Federation of Women's Clubs, about the uniqueness of the area. This conversation between Ingraham and Munroe may have been the catalyst that would one day give us Everglades National Park. Munroe would come to recommended the tract of land be donated to her organization for preservation. Momentum for the park increased with every passing year.

On December 28, 1914, with powerful politicians in tow, the Federation visited the site – traveling on a new road constructed through the hammock by the Model Land Company. A member of this party, Ms. William J. Krome, suggested that the road be named the Ingraham Highway. The suggestion was endorsed shortly thereafter by the Dade County Commission.[8]

Ingraham was able to persuade Flagler's widow, Mary, to donate 1,000 acres of Paradise Key to the Federation. The state matched this grant with an additional 1,000 acres. On November 22, 1916, 150 automobiles traversed the Ingraham Highway for the dedication of Royal Palm, Florida's first state park.[9]

The Ingraham Highway would subsequently be extended to reach all the way to Cape Sable and the tiny fishing village of Flamingo. This would eventually become the main drive through Everglades National Park. The national park plotted a more scenic course through the park and constructed a new park road in 1956 which is still in use today.

Marjory Stoneman Douglas Wilderness
In 1997, the U.S. Congress renamed the 1,302,000-acre Wilderness Preserve in Everglades National Park in honor of the "Grande Dame of the Everglades." In 1947, Marjory Stoneman Douglas wrote *The Everglades: River of Grass* – a book that would come to champion the 'Glades and reveal its many hidden wonders to the world.

Marjory began as a journalist for her father Frank Stoneman's *Miami Herald* in 1915 and knew Ernest Coe. She campaigned for many social issues but had a legacy of environmental awareness from her father who had fought against drainage of the 'Glades as early as 1906. Her message was "water is the key".[10]

She would later form the Friends of the Everglades in 1969 to fight the development of the Jetport in Big Cypress *(see Dade-Collier Training Airport in Big Cypress National Preserve)*, an influential organization dedicated to the proper stewardship of the "River of Grass".[11] She continued to author numerous titles that extolled the virtues of South Florida. Nearly until her death at the age of 108, Douglas continued an active life of advocacy on behalf of this natural treasure. Following her passing, her ashes were scattered across the wilderness she fought so tirelessly to protect.

Everglades National Park

Royal Palm Visitor Center
Long before the establishment of Everglades National Park, there was Royal Palm State Park. Originally designated in 1916 as Florida's first state park, the nearly 2000-acre parcel sought to protect one of the largest tree islands of the Everglades, Paradise Key. The area was named for the many stately royal palms, *Roystonea elata*, that pierced through the canopy of the immense hammock.[12] *See also Ingraham Highway.*

Shark Valley Visitor Center
Located on Tamiami Trail (US-41) about 35 miles west of downtown Miami, this center has a 15-mile tram and bicycle path which takes visitors through the heart of Shark Valley, for which it is named. *See also Shark Valley.*

GEOGRAPHIC FEATURES

Alligator Bay (Florida Bay)
No written record exists to relate the background of this particular moniker, but given the prevalence of American alligators throughout South Florida, it is not difficult to surmise an explanation. *See also Alligator Point.*

Alligator Bay (Ten Thousand Islands)
Loren "Totch" Brown lived all of his years in and around what is now Everglades National Park. His family moved frequently along the South Florida coast from Miami to Ft. Myers. Often, the Browns settled on uninhabited tracts of land deep within the recesses of the Ten Thousand Islands.

Totch recalled setting out one evening from their home on Opossum Key for an alligator hunt. He wrote, "We went up to Gator Bay and camped at the mouth of Gator Bay Creek. It got its name, Dad said, from a wild alligator no one could kill."[13]

Parents are fully aware of the accuracy of many of the "explanations" we offer our inquisitive children. Thus, it is unsure whether or not this information is factual. Still, it remains the only noted account for the name of this bay. And given corroborating information about "foxy gators", the story may not be so far-fetched. *See also East Fox Lake.*

Alligator Creek
Glen Simmons recounted once finding the remains of several skinned alligators at the mouth of this creek and states that such occurrences happened often. At one time, a road spanned between the mouth of the creek and Flamingo and afforded easy access for launching boats. The creek served as the primary avenue of entry for a chain of lakes further inland.[14]

The drainage efforts of the 1950s encouraged the encroachment of more saline waters inland from the coast. Not surprisingly, the flora and fauna of these coastal areas have changed as well.[15] Prior to the effects of canals and pumps, the lakes accessible through Alligator Creek did, in fact, teem with its freshwater-dwelling namesake. The waterway was likely a favorite of sportsmen and gator hunters alike.

Alligator Point

The American alligator, *Alligator mississippiensis*, is a common resident of South Florida. They are found in abundance throughout the freshwater environments of Everglades National Park and normally do not inhabit the marine waters of the coast, unlike the American crocodile *(see Crocodile Point)*.

Occasionally, however, a wayward alligator will make the journey towards the salty waters of the shore. This typically occurs during spring, when individuals trek beyond their normal ranges in search of a mate. A scan of recent news reports leaves no dearth of examples where large alligators were removed after suddenly appearing at public beaches.

While it is unclear how this particular spit of land earned its moniker, one can be certain that, at some point in time, an alligator maneuvered his ponderous bulk to this location.

Anhinga Trail

The anhinga, *Anhinga anhinga,* is a bird frequently encountered in the wetlands of the Everglades. Sporting predominantly black plumage with hints of white along the tail and back, they will often perch themselves with wings spread wide to capture the warmth of the sun. The webbed feet of the birds suggest they are highly aquatic, diving into shallow waters to retrieve their favorite meal – fish skewered on their sharply pointed beaks! Watching a successful hunter toss his prey into the air and swallow his meal head-first is always a fascinating spectacle.

Visitors to the park between January and May will understand why this trail gets its name. During these months, anhingas will readily use the abundance of pond apple trees in the area to build nests and rear their young. During times of peak activity, the area will be filled with the sounds of rapid, high-pitched clicking – the sounds of young looking to attract the attention of their parents for a meal! Nests are usually plentiful and easy to spot, making this one of the most popular wildlife viewing areas. The Trail is easily accessible by car and the boardwalk is roughly half a mile long.

Arsenic Bank
This stretch of shallows envelops the Arsnicker Keys. *See also Arsenicker Key in Biscayne National Park.*

Barnes Key
While both an island and a sound share this moniker, nothing appears to be known about their mysterious namesake.

Bear Lake, Bear Lake Canoe Trail
The first Florida black bear ever collected was from Key Biscayne in 1858. This individual became the type specimen for a new subspecies, *Ursus americanus floridana.* The range of this particular subspecies extends well to the north into Georgia, but accounts of its occurrence in South Florida are scant. Evidence suggests, however, that bears were found throughout the southern tip of the peninsula and perhaps the islands of the keys.[16]

It is entirely plausible, therefore, that this body of water was dubbed "Bear Lake" due to a particular occurrence or a frequency of sightings. But Willard Dilley, a former ranger from Everglades National Park, provides evidence of perhaps an alternate explanation.

In 1954, the State game commission offered the park several Florida black bears, which the superintendent accepted eagerly. The bears had been trapped on a ranch in North Florida, and were driven down individually to Everglades by park rangers. Northwest Cape had been agreed upon as a release site, as it provided ample food and fresh water, as well as a considerable distance to prevent escape! Furthermore, Ralph Maxwell states that there were bears all through this country at one time.[17]

At Coot Bay, the bears were placed upon boats and ferried three-to-four hours to the release site. Presumably, they would have passed near Bear Lake and, perhaps, given rise to its current moniker.[18]

The 11.5 mile trail takes visitors to the northern banks of Bear Lake and beyond.

Big Key
When this island is considered alongside the adjacent Samphire Keys, it comprises the largest of the bunch, hence the name. Charles Brooksfield christened this island during one of his many aerial surveys of Florida Bay.[19]

Big Lostmans Bay
This large bay is located just east of Lostmans River. *See also Lostmans River.*

Big Sable Creek
Prior to the dredging of canals in the area, only two creeks penetrated the interior of Cape Sable. Little Sable Creek, while not noted on most park maps, is the narrower of the two and flows southeasterly to join with Lake Ingraham. This creek, as the name suggests, is wider and allows for the passage of larger vessels.[20]

Bird Key
This small mangrove island likely earned its name for the fact that it served for some time as an active bird roost. Snowy egrets, American egrets and tricolored herons were commonly observed here in great numbers.[21]

Black Betsy Keys
Evidence does exist to suggest that this island was named for a woman who resided on this island for some time.[22] Unfortunately, she has remained an enigma, as few details have been recorded.

Blackwater Sound
It is presently unclear why this body of water should bear this particular name. However, one might conjecture that it came about as a result of a profusion of "black water". In the past, the Florida Keys have suffered periodic incidents where suspected algae blooms have rendered the water a variety of unusual shades colors. On rare occasions, for reasons yet unknown, coastal waters have also turned an inky black. The earliest of these "blackwater events" was recorded back in 1878,[23] while the most

recent took place in 2002.[24] This phenomenon has been associated with massive fish kills and the loss of living coral.

While present-day visitors to this body of water may not find anything unusual, one could speculate that a similar "blackwater event" may have given rise to its current name.

Bob Allen Keys

These islands were named for an Audubon researcher by the name of Robert Porter Allen. Beginning in 1939, Allen spent several years in the vicinity of these keys studying the living habits of the Roseate Spoonbill. The findings of his meticulous research were later published in 1942, and served to expand our understanding of this magnificent species. He would later relate his experiences here in his acclaimed book, *Flame Birds*.[25] In 1964, the National Park Service bestowed a posthumous honor on this dedicated researcher by naming these three islands for him.[26]

Bob Keys

Who or what this moniker is meant to commemorate remains a mystery at this time.

The Boggies

This series of creeks serves as an often treacherous passageway between Blackwater Sound and Florida Bay. The profusion of mangroves that grow along these narrow corridors deposits a large amount of detritus, which settles to the bottom and slowly decays to create a formidable layer of thick, viscous mud.

During a journey through the Everglades area in 1896, Hugh Willoughby describes his venture through The Boggies as such, "With a light wind we sailed across Blackwater Sound, which is a pretty sheet of water nearly circular, and about four miles in diameter, taking a course nearly west, in order to find the opening which leads into the Bay of Florida, ... a rather difficult place to get a sailboat through, as the bottom is so soft that a pole pushes in to its full length."[27]

Boggy Key

While no documentation remains to provide the specific origins of this moniker, a plausible explanation can be easily surmised. Anyone who has ever walked among the mangroves of South Florida might likely wonder why every island is not so named. These forests produce an enormous amount of detritus in the waters that surround them. Decomposition of these materials is slow, producing over time a layer of thick muck often several feet deep. While these areas pose little difficulty to marine life, they can prove quite challenging for people to traverse.

Bottle Key

For reasons unknown, this island was formerly known as Bottlepoint Key. However, during an aerial survey in the 1930s, it became evident that the island itself was shaped like a bottle. The "point" was subsequently dropped, leaving its present moniker.[28]

Bradley Key

Charles Brookfield suggested that this tiny island be named in honor of Guy Bradley, the first warden appointed to protect the rookeries of Cape Sable.[29] Bradley was commissioned as a game officer for the Audubon Society in 1902. Only three years later, he was killed in the line of duty while protecting a rookery from poachers. The alleged gunman, Walter Smith, gunned down Bradley near the Oyster Keys on July 8, 1905.[30] While Smith would later be acquitted of the crime, the slain officer was hailed as a "martyr to millinery". Bradley's sacrifice would force the fashion industry to its knees and spell the eventual end of the plume trade.[31] *See also Cuthbert Lake.*

Broad Creek

It has been noted that this particular body of water is relatively wider than other creeks nearby, thereby likely giving rise to its current name.[32]

Broad River, Broad River Chickee
This river has no doubt been christened due to its most notable feature. Travelers here have noted how the river widens considerably upstream, providing mariners with a sheltered anchorage.[33]

Brush Keys
Some explanations are beautiful for their simplicity. These islands were named for their heavily vegetated understories.[34]

Buchanan Keys
These keys were likely named for then-President James Buchanan by the United States Coast and Geodetic Survey in 1856, during the midst of the Third Seminole War.[35] The nearby Peterson Keys provide a bit more evidence to support this claim. They were formerly known as the Bowlegs Keys, a reference to Billy Bowlegs, famed Seminole leader of the Third Seminole War and Buchanan antagonist.[36]

Buoy Key
Once named for a Negro charcoal burner and fisherman who resided there, this island had been known previously as Commodore Key. However, its current moniker was born in the wake of the Hurricane of 1926. The violent storm washed a large, metal buoy ashore, which was later salvaged and used for a freshwater cistern at Flamingo.[37]

Buttonwood Canal
This waterway was named by the national park's first superintendent, Dan Beard, who originally wanted the waterway to be called Buttonwood Creek. The waterway was originally dug as a spur of the old Homestead Canal in 1922. In the late 1950s it was widened, deepened and extended to Coot Bay.[38]

Buttonwood Keys
    The buttonwood, *Conocarpus erectus*, is a common shoreline tree of the South Florida coast. It has been often referred to as our fourth mangrove, due to its close association with the red, white and black mangroves. Of the tree's common name, it has been written that the globular fruit are supposed to resemble old-fashioned shoe buttons.

The buttonwood played an important role in the livelihood of early South Florida settlers. The tree could be harvested by the hundreds, piled together, and burned slowly to produce charcoal. There was a great demand for the finished product. In his time around Flamingo, Lawrence Will recounts, "About the steadiest and longest-lasting source of income was from the marketing of 'coal'. In Key West there was a steady demand for this for cooking and heating. Good buttonwood charcoal would bring $1.50 a sack, and the coal boats were the main means of contact with civilization for people of the Cape." [39]

For this reason, the buttonwood was highly prized and eagerly sought. It is entirely plausible, then, that this key derived its name from a particularly plentiful growth of the timber.

Buttonwood Sound
It is plausible to surmise that this moniker was bestowed due to the occurrence of buttonwood trees on the coasts that surround this body of water.

Buzzard Key
Two species of vultures are found abundantly in the Florida Everglades. These include the turkey vulture, *Cathartes aura*, and the black vulture, *Coragyps atratus*. Commonly known as "buzzards", they are best known for their voracious appetite for carrion. Vultures are also known to congregate in great numbers while flying, roosting, or feeding.[40] It may be assumed that this island was named for hosting such a spectacle at some point in time.

Calusa Keys
During his work with the United States Coast and Geodetic Survey, Charles Brookfield remembers informing his superior about the former presence of the Calusa Indians who once populated the keys and western coast of Florida. His Chief of Party, Lt. Madison, believed it would be appropriate to commemorate the memory of the Calusas. Hence these keys were so named.[41]

Camp Key
It has been noted that certain areas in the park were used historically as seasonal fishing camps. This appropriately named island is one such location. As may be expected, these wilderness areas afforded few amenities, though pilings did exist at this site for fishermen to dry their nets.[42]

Canepatch Campsite
At one time, this site was known as Avocado Creek. Tebeau reported that the creek flowed past a large mound that supported living avocado trees and exhibited other evidences of cultivation.[43] Ralph Maxwell, Assistant Chief Ranger of Everglades during the 1950s-1960s, reported finding only one avocado tree here, though there were also guava, banana, and lime trees in addition to sugar cane – which likely gave rise to its current moniker.[44]

Cannon Bay
Scanty records exist of a man by the name of Cannon who resided on a homestead at Possum Key.[45] He is no doubt the namesake for this tiny body of water. It has been reported that Frank Cannon and his son Jack discovered the slain body of Hannah Smith in the shallow waters of the Chatham River in 1910.[46] "Bloody Ed" Watson would later be accused of her murder, among others. *See also Watson Place Campsite.*

Cape Sable
The true origins of this name are something of a mystery.[47] In charting the coast of South Florida and the keys in the 1770s, Capt. Bernard Romans referred to this southernmost tip of the mainland as "Sandy Point", or in French, "Cape Sable".[48] However, this land mass of mangrove, coastal prairie, and white sand beaches may have derived its current moniker from the sabal palms that are found there.

Present-day visitors to the Cape can decide for themselves how this area got its name. The question is best pondered enjoying a stretch of unspoiled, sandy beach beneath the shade of a stately sabal palm.

Captain Key
While the waters of Florida Bay have been plied by a good many captains in years gone by, no evidence exists to indicate which of these skippers this mangrove island commemorates.

Carl Ross Key, Carl Ross Key Campsite
This relatively new island was forged by the fury of Hurricane Donna in 1960.[49] Previously a part of nearby Sandy Key, this newly separated land mass was named in honor of Carl Ross who was the nephew of famed Flamingo resident "Uncle Steve" Roberts. He settled here permanently in 1928 and, following the creation of Everglades National Park in 1947, worked as a captain's mate for the EPCo., the park concessionaire.[50] *See also Roberts River.*

Catfish Key
Both the hardhead catfish, *Arius felis*, and the gafftopsail catfish, *Bagre marinus*, commonly inhabit the brackish waters of Florida Bay. Most anglers consider them something to avoid and it is likely that this key was named for a profusion of these fish in the area at one time.

Cattail Lakes
Over the past century, human impacts have ushered significant changes in the area of Cape Sable. Not the least of these has been the dredging of canals, which has led to rapid coastal erosion and the intrusion of salt water far inland. It has been noted, for example, that these lakes were fresh water at one time and cattails grew on them.[51] Glen Simmons, a long-time outdoorsman in the 'Glades, corroborates this statement by recounting, "There were a good many cattails in them, but the lakes were open enough to hunt."[52]

Chatham Bend, Chatham River
This bay may have been named in honor of the coastal town of Chatham, located in Kent roughly 17 miles east of London, England. Situated on the banks of the Medway River, the borough boasts a long history as a military town. It is perhaps best known as the location of the Royal Naval Dockyard, which has produced a plethora of well-known warships, including six that bear the name *Chatham*.[53]

This location may also have been named to commemorate William Pitt, the Elder (1708-1778), otherwise known as the First Earl of Chatham. During the course of the Seven Years' War, Pitt was pivotal in establishing Britain as a military superpower. In later years, he would also become known as an unwavering champion of American states' rights.[54]

Surveyor William Gerard de Brahm is credited for naming this bay among the Ten Thousand Islands, though no evidence exists to explain his intent.[55] Whether this moniker was meant to commemorate a place or a person will forever remain a tantalizing mystery.

Chekika

Chekika was the leader of a band of renegade Indians that tormented both military forces and civilians during the Second Seminole War. Many historical accounts describe Chekika and his allies as "Spanish Indians" – likely some of the last remaining remnants of the Calusas in Florida.[56] Scholars have debated the accuracy of these accounts and questioned whether or not they may have been an isolated band of Seminoles.[57] But to his enemies, his ancestry was less important than his often-lethal influence.

In 1840, Chekika lead a deadly attack on the island of Indian Key that took the lives of seven people, one of whom was the famed botanist Dr. Henry Perrine. In response, Colonel William S. Harney set forth with a band of men in an effort to locate Chekika and avenge the massacre. Using relatively new techniques in riverine warfare, Harney's men were able to locate the hammock deep in the 'Glades where Chekika was hiding. Here they killed him and were ordered to hang his lifeless body from a tree as a warning to other Indians in the area.[58]

This dramatic tragedy unfurled on a hammock in the vicinity of the modern-day Chekika which was formerly a State Recreation Area that was deeded to the Everglades National Park. *See also Harney River.*

Chevelier Bay

Jean Chevelier lived on Opossum Key during the late 1880s and 1890s near the bay that now bears his name.[59] Known by locals of the time merely as the "old Frenchman", he was largely regarded as an eccentric naturalist, avid hunter, skilled taxidermist, and "collector of bird skins and plumes."⁶⁰ His Chevelier Corporation bought the Watson Place in 1919 for development but his plans failed.⁶¹

Chokoloskee
The Seminoles christened this area with its current moniker, which loosely translated means "old house" or "big house". The name likely refers to the island's origins as a large Indian shell mound created as a refuse pile by the southwest coast's earlier residents. The island is only 150 acres, but at its highest point stands nearly 20 feet in elevation.⁶² It was settled in the 1880s by the Santini and Smallwood families. The island is not part of the park and is still occupied by private residences.

Chokoloskee Bay
This large body of water is home to the island of Chokoloskee. In early days, the whole area, including what is now Everglades City, was referred to as Chokoloskee.

Chokoloskee Pass
This winding waterway leads boaters to the island of Chokoloskee.

Christian Point Trail
The story behind this place name remains a tantalizing mystery. No evidence has been found to indicate why this beautiful trail to Florida Bay should be given this particular moniker.

Clive Key
No information exists to explain the origins of this particular moniker.

Club Key
Charles Brooksfield worked for a time on Tavernier Key with the Airphoto Reconnaissance Group. Their mission was to identify geographic features that had not yet been identified on charts.

The work afforded Brooksfield a birds-eye view of the area. From the air he noted that a number of mangrove islands bore distinctive shapes and named them accordingly. This one, he recalled, was shaped somewhat like a war club.⁶³

Clubhouse Beach Campsite

Flagler's Model Land Company was responsible for all land transactions associated with the Florida East Coast Railroad and had surveyed Cape Sable as an alternative route for the Key West railroad. In an effort to develop the Flamingo area in the 1920s, the Model Land Company maintained a clubhouse in the vicinity of the present-day campsite. Visitors were brought here by boat from various points along the Keys Railway. The clubhouse was situated on the beach and stood tall on stilts. It boasted a long hallway down the center of the structure with five rooms on either side, as well as a large, screened porch where meals were served.[64] While the clubhouse fell to the elements over time, the area remains a popular location for overnight camping.

Cluett Key

In his book *The Cruise of the Seminole*, Vincent Gilpin recounts his expedition through the Florida Keys in the Spring of 1905. Several individuals joined him aboard the yawl-rigged sharpie, *Seminole*, including an old friend by the name of Sanford Cluett.

During a brief stay at Flamingo, the party came to meet with Audubon warden Guy Bradley, who informed them of an uncharted island near Man of War Key that was a prosperous fishing ground. Years earlier, two survey parties working the waters of Florida Bay had mistakenly thought their counterparts had recorded the tiny key, while in truth, neither had.[65] Following Bradley's suggestion, the *Seminole* soon set off for Man of War Key.

The party would eventually come to circle the entire length of the uncharted island, though the area proved unprofitable for fishing. One person did, however, come away with a trophy of sorts. While there, Sanford Cluett sketched the general location of the key on his charts and sent the information to the United States Coast and Geodetic Survey, which promptly named the island in his honor.[66]

Incidentally, it has been noted that the crew of the *Seminole* were the last "outsiders" to ever see Guy Bradley alive before his murder.[67] *See also Bradley Key.*

Coastal Prairie Trail

Everglades National Park harbors a variety of ecosystems within its borders. One of these is the "coastal prairie", a lowland community that thrives between the mud flats of Florida Bay and freshwater interior to the north. Due to the constant effects of winds and storms, growing conditions here are not favorable for most plant life. Only hardy, salt-tolerant species thrive in this environment, including a variety of succulents and cacti.

This trail takes visitors along an historic road leading out to Clubhouse Beach. The trail is 7.5 miles one way and is best attempted late in the dry season.

Comer Key

Formerly known as Pelican Key, this island was christened with its current moniker at the behest of the National Park Service. The island was named for Braxton Bragg Comer, Governor of Alabama from 1907-1911, who would frequently camp there.

According to Comer's former fishing guide, Rob Storter, the Governor and his family would arrive every March for a three or four week stay. "The Governor would get up at daybreak and give a big war whoop", wrote Storter. "That meant for everybody to get up and get ready for breakfast and start fishing".[68]

Coon Key

As a highly adaptable species, raccoons are found abundantly throughout the South Florida mainland. It has also been suggested that raccoons have probably inhabited every island in the park to which they could wade or swim.[69]

The raccoon played an important role in the economy of the 'Glades frontier. They were eagerly sought for their pelts, and were hunted in large numbers. Today, the "coon" is less appreciated for its fur than for its tenacity and intelligence. Given an opportunity, raccoons can easily figure out how to ravage the supplies of the careless visitor.

Though normally active at night, raccoons are routinely encountered during daylight hours. They remain one of the most conspicuous and charismatic members of our fauna. While specific evidence does not exist to explain the moniker bestowed upon this island, one can be sure a furry, masked bandit was likely involved. *See also Raccoon Point in Big Cypress National Preserve and Coon Point in Biscayne National Park.*

Coot Bay
This body of water became legendary for the astounding mass of bird life to be found there every winter. All manner of waterfowl utilized the shallow bay to feed. The most common of these was the American coot, *Fulica americana*, a common bird found among the shallow environments of the Everglades. This small, black bird is often found in large flocks, swimming communally with other aquatic species.[70] Historically, coots used to arrive here by the thousands, so as to form "rafts" that would seemingly occupy half of the bay's size.[71] While coots can still be seen in the park every winter, they no longer arrive in such numbers to their namesake bay.

Coot Bay Pond
This tiny pond is located east of the much larger Coot Bay. Today, a narrow channel connects Coot Bay Pond with Coot Bay. This channel was dredged in 1945 by Louis Watson, proprietor of the Watson Fish Camp that operated in the area.[72] The channel provided sportsmen easy entry into the backcountry from the road. *See also Watson River.*

Cormorant Key
The double-crested cormorant, *Phalacrocorax auritus*, is one of the more common species found around the waters of South Florida. These birds frequently roost together in large trees along the coast and along the freshwater habitats of the interior. Closely related to pelicans, the cormorant is a highly aquatic species that feeds primarily on fish.[73] It is most probable that this island was christened for its attractiveness to large flocks of its namesake.

Corrine Key

This island represents one of the great mysteries of Florida Bay. It is unclear exactly who or what this island has been christened after.

Crab Keys

A wide diversity of crabs, including the ghost crab pictured here, inhabits the waters and shorelines of South Florida. While it is usually the commercially important species that come to mind (blue crabs, stone crabs, etc.), evidence suggests that this moniker may have served as a warning for fishermen. Stories persist of fishermen who, on certain keys, had their nets ruined by crabs when left out to dry.[74]

Crab Key Bight

Place names often result from either an outstanding landscape feature, a specific individual, or a specific event. This island's moniker comes from the latter. Sam Hamilton, Sr. and James Frank Hamilton lost their fishing nets to blue crabs here in 1923. The current name seems to commemorate this unfortunate event.[75]

Crane Keys

South Florida boasts a number of birds with white plumage, stilt legs and long, thin necks. Casual observers will often refer to these informally as "cranes". In truth, several different species of herons and egrets share these characteristics, so it is difficult to say for which in particular this key was named. Because these species will often roost together or nest together in large rookeries, the island may have been dubbed for a collection of "cranes", rather than just one.

Crate Key

While no official explanation exists, one might guess that this island was named for the one-time presence of crate-like traps. However, it is commonly known that the islands of Florida Bay were used for more dubious activities, for which true crates may have been present.

Crocodile Point

The waters of South Florida represent the northernmost range of the American crocodile, *Crocodylus acutus*, which has a pointier snout than the alligator *(see Alligator Point)* and thrives in brackish, coastal waters.

Historically, these impressive reptiles populated the southernmost coastlines of the peninsula in a contiguous stretch from Juno Beach to Tampa. In recent times, coastal development has reduced the crocodiles' potential habitat significantly, though populations still thrive in the waters of Everglades National Park. Why this particular spit of land bears the unique distinction, however, is something of a mystery.

Curlew Key

The use of common names in describing flora and fauna is always problematic, as often these may be regional in nature or may be different among cultures. Over time, these names may undergo changes or disappear altogether.

A sampling of field guides for the birds of South Florida, illustrates the great diversity of names applied to a single species of bird. The long-billed curlew, *Numenius americanus,* is also known as the "sickle-bill". The whimbrel, *Numenius phaeopus*, is often called the "Hudsonian curlew". And the willet, *Catoptrophorus semipalmatus*, is known by a variety of monikers including the "stone curlew", "bill-willie", "white-wing curlew", and the "pill-willet".[76] It would appear that any bird with a distinctly curved beak has, at one point or another, been referred to as a "curlew".

The white ibis is one of the park's most ubiquitous and historically useful species. Because it sports a curved bill, it should not be surprising that many early explorers in the area referred to these birds as "curlews".[77] Charles William Pierce, in recounting a five-month expedition in 1885 along the eastern coast and the Florida Keys, frequently describes hunting "curlews". It is probable that the white ibis, which use many of these keys as rookeries, was that to which he referred.[78]

Several early settlers also recalled "curlews" and "Chokoloskee chickens" as an abundant and savory food, no doubt in reference to the plentiful white ibis of the area.[79,80]

Cuthbert Lake
This inland body of water located just east of West Lake is named for the plume hunter who made his fortune there. For the forty years or so between 1870 and 1910, the breeding plumes of herons and egrets were in intense demand for the adornment of women's hats. At the peak of this craze, these feathers were worth their weight in gold. In 1890, at the lake that bears his name, a hunter by the name of Cuthbert found a bustling rookery of egrets. His initial slaughter earned him $1,800 – a veritable fortune for the time![81]

It has been noted that, based upon the asking price of plumes at the time, it would have taken more than four pounds of feathers to amass such earnings.[82] The number of birds killed to attain this number of feathers must have been staggering, and it is known that the rookery was a favorite spot for subsequent plume hunters looking to replicate Cuthbert's success. As one might imagine, the productivity of the rookery has sharply declined. But to this day, the rookery remains active, and according to recent surveys, hosts nesting cormorants, egrets, and wood storks.[83] *See also Bradley Key.*

Dads Bay
In recording the oral histories of Flamingo residents during the early 1900s, Jean Taylor writes of a well-known maker of moonshine in the area. "Dad Albrecht" was the main source of liquor for the tiny community of Flamingo. It was commonly known among the residents that he would hide his stash on various little islands.[84]

Flamingo is, however, far removed from the location of Dads Bay. It is unlikely, therefore that Albrecht serves as the namesake of this body of water. Rather, it is more plausible that the bay commemorates the memory of some unknown patriarch of the Ten Thousand Islands.

Darwin's Place Campsite

Arthur Leslie Darwin retired to a small plot of land on Opossum Key in 1945. Leading a reclusive life, he farmed on roughly six acres and occasionally sold his produce in Everglades City. Arthur is perhaps best remembered for claiming he was a fifth-generation descendent of the famed evolutionist Charles Darwin. Prior to the park's expansion in 1989, Darwin held the distinction of being the last private landholder to reside in the borders of Everglades National Park. He continued to live on Possum Key until his passing in 1977, reportedly at an age of 88.[85] *See also Opposum Key.*

Davis Cove

This body of water in eastern Florida Bay is likely named for Raoul Davis, a crocodile hunter and farmer of the area.[86] Prior to 1910, both Raoul and his son, Rollin, spent several years farming on a plot of land between Davis Creek and Joe Bay.

Rollin would recount in later years that a female crocodile would return every year to build a nest at their camp.[87] Historically, northeastern Florida Bay seemed exceptionally hospitable to crocodiles, and in turn, crocodile hunters. Today, several of the bays located here are closed to public access, serving as critical habitat for this threatened species. *See also Joe Bay.*

Dead Terrapin Key

While no records exist to explain this morbid moniker, one can only surmise that, at some point in time, one (or many) expired turtles were discovered upon this tiny island. *See also Terrapin Bay.*

Deer Key

While the white-tailed deer, *Odocoileus virginia*, is a common resident of the upland environments of the mainland, it is not a creature commonly encountered among the islands of Florida Bay. Still, it has been written that one could reasonably expect to have found them here at some time, since it is located so close to shore.[88] After all, the Florida Key deer, *Odocoileus virginia clavium*, is a related subspecies that is known to be particularly aquatic and adept at migrations between islands.

EVERGLADES NATIONAL PARK

Derelict Key
It is not surprising that an island would bear this name. Much has been written regarding the outlaws, brigands, and ruffians who sought refuge in the wilderness of the Everglades.[89] The term "derelict" has previously been used to reference some of the more nefarious among them.[90]

Accounts do exist of numerous transients squatting upon the islands of Florida Bay, often using their remote locales for unscrupulous industries.[91] Consequently, the specific "derelict" for whom this island is named will most likely remain a mystery.

Dildo Key, Dildo Key Bank
This island derives its moniker from its profusion of a particular species of cactus that bears the same name.[92] The dildo cactus, *Acanthocereus tetragonus*, thrives along the mangrove coastline of extreme southern Florida.[93] The plant's common name is derived from its unique shape. Incidentally, famed botanist John Kunkel Small notes of this species that "the seedling plant starts with a slender, several ribbed shoot."[94]

Duck Key
Many different varieties of ducks have been observed inhabiting the waters of South Florida.[95] Recent years reveal far fewer numbers than were seen historically. Though the reason for this decline is still unclear, it is probable that man's manipulation of natural water flows over the past century have no doubt played a role. It is also probable that this mangrove key derived its name from a profusion of one or more species of duck that called the island home, though today there are few to be found.

Duck Rock Cove
Many years back, the key that lies in the middle of this body of water consisted of little more than an island of bare rock with a lake in the center. Ducks would flock here to feed and the area became known as a popular spot for hunting waterfowl, thus becoming known as "Duck Rock".[96]

Over time, favorable conditions led to the thick growth of vegetation on the island. The resulting forest served for many years as one of the most prolific roosting sites for ibis, herons, cormorants, pelicans, and roseate spoonbills to name a few. But the spectacle was not to last. In 1960, Hurricane Donna stripped the island nude once more.[97] Today, it stands as it did early in the century, a bare mound of rock.

Dump Keys

The author has heard two very different theories as to why these islands have been christened as such. The first comes from a longtime resident of the area, who asserts that at one time, racks were present on these keys where local fishermen would "dump" their nets to dry.[98]

A second theory states that at one time, these islands were formerly known as the "Shit Keys" and were a popular place for fishermen to seek scatological relief. Following the acquisition of this area by the Federal government, however, a more suitable moniker was deemed necessary and the islands were given their current name.[99]

Eagle Key

The bald eagle, *Haliaeetus leucocephalus*, is a common year-round resident of Florida. They are frequently found residing near open bodies of freshwater and along the coast.[100] They are known to nest among the mangroves of the Everglades and it is most probable that the island was named for a pair or individual that was spotted here.

The golden eagle, *Aquila chrysaetos*, is a far rarer species that has been encountered only a handful of times in the Everglades.[101] There is a chance, therefore, that the island may have also derived its moniker from an isolated observation here.

East Cape Campsite

Three sandy points adorn the southwestern coast of the Cape Sable land mass. Each is named for its geographic location relative to each other. As the name implies, this point lies furthest east and closest to the former town of Flamingo.

East Cape Canal

This man-made waterway was dug in 1922 and derives its name from its proximity to East Cape.[102] The canals dredged around Cape Sable have been blamed for extensive degradation of the area. Originally less than 20 feet across, unyielding erosion along its banks has rendered this canal to presently exceed 200 feet in width.[103]

As the ocean continues to tear inward, many of the formerly freshwater haunts of the Cape are suffering greatly from salt water intrusion. The future may see restoration efforts to stem the damage from canals such as these around the Cape.

East Fox Lake

Just northwest of Bear Lake lie several bodies of water named consecutively East Fox Lake, Middle Fox Lake, and Little Fox Lake. In his book, *A Dredgeman of Cape Sable*, Lawrence Will quipped, "I reckon that names were getting scarce when the original discoverer had to name them." Will goes on to mention that the lakes were "fairly fresh", rendering these lakes important sources of water for local wildlife.[104]

The fauna of the region does include both the red, *Vulpes vulpes*, and gray fox, *Urocyon cineroargenteus*.[105] It is plausible that sightings of foxes in the proximity of these lakes could have given rise to their current names.

However, long-time Everglades explorer Glen Simmons says the lakes derived their current moniker because the alligators here were "foxy". Being quite limited in access, these lakes probably harbored alligators that were quite skittish to the presence of people. For Simmons, hunting alligators at night usually required the use of a carbide lantern. The eyes of alligators nearby would "catch fire", or reflect back, making the reptiles easy to spot and kill. But of the "foxy" gators of these lakes, Simmons recalls, "'Twas said that they wouldn't hold fire long enough to get a shot at them."[106]

East Key

While no official documentation exist to corroborate this claim, it is most likely that this island was named for its position in relation to the coastline of the Florida Keys.

Eco Pond Trail

Long-time visitors to the park will recall that this roughly half-mile long trail formerly circled a large, shallow water lagoon. This man-made body of water served many years as a filtration/settlement pond for waste generated by the nearby facilities of Flamingo. This advanced wastewater system was designed as a sustainable, earth-friendly method of disposal. Perhaps as evidence to its success, hordes of wildlife could often be found utilizing the lagoon during typical winter days.

Over the past few years, the completion of a new wastewater treatment facility in Flamingo has rendered the pond obsolete. Coupled with the effects of both Hurricanes Katrina and Wilma in 2005, the trail is a very different experience today than it was only a few years ago!

End Key

Lying at the north end of a long stretch of keys, this island derived its moniker as the terminus of the string of Coon and Buttonwood Keys.[107]

Ernest Coe Campsite

This campsite is name for Ernest F. Coe, the "Father" of Everglades National Park. *See also Ernest F. Coe Visitor Center.*

Ficus Pond

Numerous species of *Ficus* can be found around South Florida, most of which are ornamentals used for landscaping. In the wilds of the Everglades, however, only two native species are found: the strangler fig, *Ficus aurea*, and the short-leaf fig, *Ficus citrifolia*. Of the two, the strangler fig is far more common.

The strangler fig derives its name from its peculiar growth habit. After having eaten fruit from this tree, birds will often deposit seeds in the crowns of other trees where they perch. These seeds will often germinate and begin to grow skyward, using the host tree for support. As the young fig grows skyward, its will send aerial roots down around the tree and eventually anchor in the ground below. These roots grow larger and more numerous as the tree gains size. Eventually, the fig will out-compete its host for resources.

This pond is no doubt named for the numerous specimens of strangler fig that persist here. Observant visitors who peer within their hollow trunks can see where their respective host trees one stood.

First Bay
Travelers up the Lostmans River found themselves entering and passing through a string of large bays. These were named for the order in which they were encountered traveling inland from the Gulf. Once around Lostmans Key you would encounter First Bay, followed later by Second Bay, Third Bay. The aptly-named Lostmans Five Bay represents the fifth major body of water to be encountered on the journey.

First National Bank
Famed naturalist Roger Hammer attributes this name to the residents of Flamingo, who demonstrated a genuine sense of humor in designating this shallow body of water.[108]

Flamingo
The small fishing village of Flamingo received its official name in 1893 when the handful of residents requested the establishment of a post office. An official name was necessary to establish the branch and Flamingo was born![109]

The moniker has greatly confused residents ever since. There is scant evidence that wild flamingos nested anywhere in Florida,[110] though they did appear periodically around the waters of the extreme southern coast to feed in sizeable flocks, sometimes estimated to be a thousand strong.[111] Still, spotting these colorful migrants from the Caribbean was a relatively rare occurrence. The birds continue to elude most visitors today, leaving many to wonder why the area bears the name of "Flamingo".

Florida Bay
Providing perhaps the very definition of unimaginative redundancy, this bay is located in Florida and has therefore been christened "Florida Bay".[112]

Frank Key

In his book, *A Dredgeman of Cape Sable*, Lawrence E. Will recounts his work as a dredge operator building the Homestead Canal. During his time around Flamingo, Will became familiar with many of the pioneer families that called the area home in the early 1900s. One of these were the Irwins, one of whom lent his name to this particular key. In his book, Will writes that "Frank Irwin homesteaded Frank's Key in 1921 but lived there only 14 months. He contracted to clear right-of-way for our canal and with the proceeds he built a house in Homestead."[113]

Garfield Bight

It is currently unclear who is honored in the christening of this particular landscape feature. It has been suggested, however, that this name was applied by a survey team in the 1930s.[114]

Florida is rife with tributes to former United States presidents. Roadways, islands, rivers and forts have been named to honor the likes of Reagan, Buchanan, Taylor, and Jefferson. It is plausible, therefore, that this spit of land was named in honor of assassinated President James A. Garfield (1831-1881). His abbreviated term of office yielded little action directly affecting the South Florida coast, so it is questionable why this area would bear his name. Furthermore, this honor would have been bestowed nearly half a century posthumously.

President Garfield's son, however, was appointed Secretary of the Interior by President Roosevelt in 1907. James R. Garfield has been described as a friend to the conservation movement and a close ally to famed forester Gifford Pinchot. However, Garfield also served a short tenure of only two years, and was quickly replaced under President Taft.[115] Everglades National Park would not be dedicated for another several decades, so again it is doubtful that this area honors his memory.

Without further evidence, the individual behind this name will likely remain an unsolved mystery.

Gopher Keys (Florida Bay)

Clarence B. Moore was a self-taught archaeologist who made frequent trips along the lower western coast of South Florida looking for evidence of Indian culture. These trips continued until 1926 when his ship, *The Gopher*, was destroyed among these keys by a hurricane.[116]

Everglades National Park

Gopher Keys (Ten Thousand Islands)
While it is presently unclear why this island may have earned this moniker, one can conjecture that the islands were named for the occurrence of the gopher tortoise. This reclusive reptile is locally abundant and may have been found here at one time.

Graveyard Creek Campsite
Two stories circulate regarding the origins of this moribund moniker. Through the early 1900s, this area and its denizens lived relatively free from any formal rule of law. Frontier justice prevailed, individuals tended to their own business, and few records were ever kept. Given these circumstances, each story is both plausible to believe yet impossible to verify.

One account speaks of two pairs of brothers who resided among the Ten Thousand Islands. The Hamilton family lived on a claim along the Lostmans River[117], while the Brown brothers inhabited a camp at the mouth of the Shark River. Over time, the Browns would come to accuse two of the Hamilton brothers of stealing raccoon hides. In retribution, one of the accused caught one of his accusers and shot him dead. He then induced his brother to kill the remaining Brown in an effort to hide their crime. Both bodies were buried in the area that would later be known as Graveyard Creek. It has been said that this story only came to light when one of the Hamilton boys became inebriated and boasted of their exploits.[118]

Another story tells of the existence of a bark factory that was in the business of making tannin. Such factories did exist and operate among the Ten Thousand Islands, lending an air of authenticity to this account.[119] This particular facility (likely that of the Manetta Company), located at the mouth of the Shark River, was staffed by African-American laborers. While details remain sketchy, it is said that some of the workers died, likely in a fight among themselves, and were buried there.[120]

Everglades National Park

Gumbo Limbo Trail

The gumbo limbo, *Bursera simarouba*, is a tropical species of tree found commonly throughout the park. It is one of the area's few deciduous species, losing its leaves during our winter months, only to grow anew in the spring. Perhaps its most distinguishing feature, however, is its paper-thin, reddish-gray bark that flakes away at the slightest touch. In an environment that harbors numerous air-plants and parasites, this unusual bark seems to ensure a relatively pest-free existence.

The gumbo limbo is well adapted to life in an area prone to bad storms and hurricanes. The tree is capable of toppling over completely, taking root anew, and growing skyward from wherever it has fallen. This quality has helped it acquire fame as the "fence post tree" throughout Central and South America, where its branches are commonly harvested and planted every few feet apart to use as living fence posts.

Visitors to the Gumbo Limbo Trail will find this species growing in abundance. Careful observers will notice the conspicuous damage left from the ravaging winds of Hurricanes Andrew, Katrina, and Wilma. Among the fallen trees can be found numerous gumbo limbos – many of which continue to grow skyward even today.

Gun Rock Point

This locale will remain an intriguing enigma, as no documentation exists to explain the origins of its unusual moniker.

Harney River, Harney River Chickee

Ninety men in sixteen canoes set out westward from the mouth of the Miami River on December 4, 1840. Under the command of Colonel William S. Harney, the garrison was to avenge the raid of Indian Key only four months before. The attack, led by a fierce Indian warrior named Chekika, had killed seven people in total – including famed botanist Dr. Henry Perrine.

Following four days of working slowly through a seemingly endless drudgery of swamp and sawgrass, Colonel Harney and his men arrived at Chekika's island hideout. Never before had white soldiers been successful at pursuing the Indians through the difficult terrain. Caught by surprise, the Seminoles were easily captured. Chekika was killed, and the soldiers were ordered to hang his body at the site to serve as a warning to others.

Rather than return the same forty-mile route they had just traversed, Harney ordered his men to proceed westward, hoping to find more navigable waters. Missing the Shark River they intended to use, they happened upon the river that today bears the Colonel's name.[121] *See also Chekika.*

Hells Bay Canoe Trail, Hells Bay Chickee
Barney Parker, the first ranger in Everglades National Park, is credited with noting that this body of water was "hell to get into and hell to get out of". This sentiment would no doubt give rise to this trail's current moniker.[122]

Glen Simmons knew the Everglades long before it was a national park. Seeking to make a living from the landscape, the "gladesmen" of his time would navigate the waters of this area by skiff or dugout canoe. In recalling his exploits along this waterway, Simmons recalls that he had never before heard the name Hell's Bay Trail. "But", he noted, "we always had a job getting through from the road to the main river. This trail twisted and turned worser than any snake and was grown thick with mangroves."[123]

Henry Lake
Evidence seems to suggest that this moniker may commemorate Argyle Hendry, an alligator trapper who maintained several camps in the vicinity of the lake.[124] In the absence of contrary evidence, the current name seems to be a corruption.[125]

Hidden Lake
This picturesque three-acre lake, like so many others in the Everglades, is man-made. Commonly referred to as a "borrow pit", it is the end result of systematic digging for fill material. In all likelihood the soil and rock

taken from this lake was used in the creation of the Old Ingraham Highway or Royal Palm Lodge.

This body of water was formerly known as "Donut Lake" due to its location in the "Hole-in-the-Donut" (HID) area of the park. The HID is a former farming area that, owing to its disturbed state, had been invaded by an exotic species called Brazilian pepper, *Schinus terebinthifolius*. The plant grows so thickly it crowds out competing vegetation and forms a virtual monoculture. In this case, the Brazilian pepper had grown so copiously as to completely "hide" the location of the lake – giving rise to its current moniker.[126]

Highland Beach Campsite

Because it lies just south of the mouth of Lostmans River, this area was formerly known as Lostmans Beach. Tebeau describes this site as a "picturesque little sand beach with a bit of higher land behind it." It would seem evident, therefore, how this area came to be given its current name.[127]

Hog Key Campsite

Settler Richard Hamilton purchased a claim on this island and endeavored to raise hogs there. It was soon discovered that wild individuals bore inedible meat owing to their diet of oysters and crabs. The hogs were later penned and were given feed that encouraged a more favorable flavor.[128]

Descendents of Hamilton's hogs persist on the island to this day. They pose a significant challenge for the park's resource managers as their rooting behavior is very destructive. *See also Mormon Key Campsite.*

Homestead Canal

In 1916, local landowners of the Cape Sable and Royal Palm area successfully lobbied the Everglades Drainage District to form the Homestead Sub-Drainage District. One of the first projects undertaken by the new agency was the extension of a road and canal from the town of Homestead to the coastal hamlet of Flamingo.[129]

The town, drainage district, and canal were all appropriately named, as collectively they would open the area to a new generation of settlers.

House Hammock Bay

This bay served as a home to an industrious pair of brothers, Bill and Dan House, who collectively embodied the typical lifestyle of most residents in the area. The brothers lived and farmed on a shell mound, to which they had dug a small ditch to facilitate access.[130]

The pair had years of experience around the waterways of the area, and were often hired as guides by sportsmen and hide dealers.[131] But perhaps their most lucrative venture reared its head during prohibition. W.J. Rutledge, working on construction of the Tamiami Trail, recounted that the pair were known to smuggle liquor from Nassau and sell it to the laborers at a premium. During one particularly bad rain storm, Rutledge recalls that roughly 60 percent of their dynamite was damaged and was subsequently sold to the House brothers. They later hired Rutledge to dynamite this bay to better accommodate their vessels.[132]

Huston River, Huston Bay

This particular moniker represents one of the great mysteries in the nomenclature of Everglades National Park. The name "Huston" has been ascribed to one river and two bays among the Ten Thousand Islands. And while much has been written about life around these areas, little has been suggested to explain the origins of this appellation.

Indian Key, Indian Key Pass

Most, if not all, of the islands of Everglades National Park have likely figured into the story of aboriginal man in South Florida. This island's moniker is rather general, and no evidence has been found to verify whether it commemorates an individual, tribe, or specific event. The Pass is a natural channel east of the key.

Jack Daniels Key

Everglades City has often been described as a "quaint little drinking village with a fishing problem." Given that sort of notoriety, it would seem obvious that this island was named for one of the more popular libations. However, the Daniels family of Everglades City is firmly established, with Jack being a well-regarded local fisherman and guide.[133]

Jim Foot Key
No records exist to provide details on the namesake for this island.

Joe Bay
William Edmund Dickinson, curator for the Milwaukee Public Museum, recounted a 1942 expedition to capture a live American crocodile for display. During this trip, he refers to this large body of water in east Florida Bay as "Alligator Joe's Bay". He further notes the remains of "Joe's crocodile corral" located on one of the bay's small islands.[134] Glen Simmons recalls, "There was another [crocodile] pen in the middle of Joe Bay, which was probably named for Alligator Joe who later had a tourist trap showplace in Miami."[135]

Joe Kemp Key
This island bears the name of its original homesteader. Sadly, little is known about Joe Kemp except that his land was sold by his heirs to Flamingo resident Coleman Irwin in 1907.[136]

Joe River, Joe River Chickee
One record seems to indicate that this river may have been named for a Joe Williams.[137] Unfortunately, little more is known about this individual or his relation to the area.

Johnson Key
An Indian mound located near the headwaters of the Lostman's River bears this same name, and it has been suggested that they were named for the same person.[138] Unfortunately, little remains to give us more detail about this individual.

Kingston Key Campsite
No documentation exists to explain the origins of this moniker although there was a sportsman of that name who bought land in Everglades City in 1911.[139]

Lake Ingraham
This large lake on the southwestern edge of Cape Sable has been formerly known as both "Whitewater Lake" and "Nine Mile Lake". Its recent designation as Lake Ingraham serves to honor the memory of the president of Henry Flagler's Model Land Company, James E. Ingraham.[140] *See also Ingraham Highway.*

Lake Key
This key was named for the island's nearly-enclosed lake.[141] It is interesting to note that many of the keys in Florida Bay boast large lagoons in their centers. Given their location, it is not surprising that these "lakes" are comprised primarily of brackish water. During our daily summer rains, however, a lens of freshwater often forms over the lagoons. These areas provide an important source of fresh water for island wildlife and may have been used by early pioneers.

Lane Bay Chickee
The Oxford English Dictionary defines a "lane" as a narrow passage, or channel.[142] This definition holds true for this locale. Access to the campsite from Whitewater Bay mandates navigating through a shallow, narrow creek.

Lard Can Campsite
The unsightly name for this campsite actually stems from the utility of these large containers. During the early 1900s, hunting parties that made forays into the 'Glades would often use fifty or one hundred pound lard cans as water-proof storage for their supplies.[143] Often purchased for around 10 cents a piece, the cans boasted tight-fitting lids, rendering them the perfect "suitcases" for travel through the area.[144] Two or three might be used at a time – one to carry clothing and bedding and the others to carry miscellaneous provisions.[145] Once emptied, the canisters could also be used for collecting any number of spoils or as a still.[146]

It has been noted that some individuals would continually return to favored campsites. Non-perishable items would often be stored in lard cans and left behind to be used on future expeditions.[147] It is likely that this area served many years as a favorite base camp and was well fortified with such containers.

Last Huston Bay
This bay likely derives its name from its position as the last major body of water encountered while ascending the Huston River prior to reaching the Chatham River. *See also Huston River.*

Little Blackwater Sound
This bay lies directly northwest of a much larger body of water by the same name. *See also Blackwater Sound.*

Little Fox Lake
This body of water is the smallest of the three Fox Lakes. *See also East Fox Lake.*

Little Madeira Bay
The banks of this body of water, located just north of Madeira Bay, were also rich in mahogany. *See also Madeira Bay.*

Little Rabbit Key Campsite
This campsite is located on one of the smaller in a collection of keys by the same name. *See also Rabbit Keys.*

Little Shark River
This waterway of far narrower scope lies just to the south of Shark River to which it connects. *See also Shark River.*

Lonesome Camp
The origins of this place name remain mired in mystery.

Long Lake
This moniker represents the epitome of simple nomenclature. It aptly describes the longest body of water in the chain of lakes that stretch between Alligator Creek and West Lake.

Long Pine Key Trail
This location derives its name not from the length of the pine trees nor from the Trail, but for how far the forest extends. Historically, the stand of pines that graced this upland area seemed to go on for an eternity. On a tour of Royal Palm with Dr. John Gifford in 1937, Allen Andrews wrote of the area, "This strand, I am informed, is some thirty miles long and extends across the lower peninsula almost to the Gulf Coast."[148]

Long Sound
Spanning a distance of roughly four miles, this sound seems appropriately named. It is interesting to note, however, that nearby Little Madeira Sound and Joe Bay are comparable in size. Why this particular body of water should earn this moniker is perhaps owing only to a lack of any other distinctive feature.

Lopez River, Lopez River Campsite
In 1890, Gregorio Lopez settled in the Ten Thousand Islands on the banks of this waterway. Lopez, an immigrant from Spain, soon had a son, Alfonso.[149] The Lopez family continued to dwell on the banks of this river for two generations.[150]

Lostmans Five Bay, Lostmans Five Bay Campsite
This small bay lies at the head of the Lostmans River, and is the fifth major bay to be encountered when traveling up river from the Gulf. *See also First Bay.*

Lostmans River, Lostmans Key
In his book *Man in the Everglades*, Charlton W. Tebeau best explains the complexities of this river's disputed origins:

"Lostmans River is sometimes called Lossman's or Lawsman' River; differences in spelling arise from conflicting stories about the origin of the name. One theory is that it was meant to mark a significant proper name. David Graham Copeland thought it might be a corruption of 'Lawson's' from the surgeon general [Thomas Lawson] who led the reconnaissance expedition there in the Seminole Wars."

"Several other versions suggest it may have been named after a lost man or men. One story tells of five soldiers at Key West who hired a

Captain Jocelyn to take them up the coast to Punta Rassa. Though they were in civilian clothes, the captain suspected them of being deserters because they hid in the hold of his sloop. He put them off at the river and told them about a sawmill back in the woods where they might hide and work."

Over the years, encounters in this area have helped perpetuate this moniker. "William Smith Allen, while on route to Key West, saw someone waving a white cloth from ashore. He found three sailors (not five soldiers) who had jumped ship at Key West and had hired a man to take them to the mainland. When the boatman saw smoke on the horizon towards Key West and suspected pursuit by the Navy, he had put them ashore three days before. Allen had entered their names in his log as John, Bill, and Sam Lostman – hence Lostman's Key and Lostman's River."[151]

The tiny key lies at the mouth of the river.

Low Key
Most of the islands in Florida Bay rise only a few inches above sea level. Given that fact, it is curious why this island would be so recognized.

Lower Arsnicker Keys
Of the group of "Arsnicker" keys in the park, these are situated furthest south. *See also Arsenicker Key in Biscayne National Park.*

Lumber Key
It is likely that this island received its current name for an abundance of commercially valuable trees. *See also Wood Key.*

Madeira Bay
The West Indian mahogany, *Swietenia mahagoni*, is a tropical tree that grows commonly along the coastline of extreme South Florida. This species, often called "madeira", was most prolific along the stretch of mangrove forest extending from Flamingo to this bay.[152]

Madeira Bay, in particular, was recognized as having a remarkably dense concentration of mahogany.[153] Prized for its strong, richly-colored wood, the tree was heavily sought after and the reason for much prospecting along the coast.

Mahogany Hammock Trail

During the park's early years, there was no spur from the main park road to take visitors to this amazing hammock. Rather, it was necessary for visitors to hike a full two-and-a-half miles through the backcountry to find what was protected in this subtropical forest. Hidden in this hammock for years was the largest mahogany tree, *Swietenia mahogani*, in the United States. This "champion" tree measured twelve feet six inches in circumference at breast height, stood seventy-five feet tall, and had a crown that spread seventy-five feet.[154]

Due perhaps to their inaccessibility, the large trees of this hammock escaped the saws of the lumbermen.[155] However, they could not escape the wrath of Mother Nature. Hurricane Andrew took a heavy toll here in 1992, felling a number of the taller specimens, including the champ.

Man of War Key, Man of War Channel

The Magnificent Frigatebird is a common resident of the South Florida coastline. Otherwise known as the Man-o'-War Bird, these impressive scavengers boast a wingspan of over seven feet and bear a distinctive forked tail.

Prior to its destruction by Hurricane Donna in 1960, visitors to Man of War Key could observe a flock of these enormous birds circling high overhead in search of food.[156]

Historical accounts seem to also suggest that Man-o'-War birds may have also nested in the area. Charles William Pierce, in recounting his five-month expedition through the coastal waters of the southern mainland and the keys in 1885, makes mention of happening upon an island near Barnes Sound where Man-o-War birds were nesting. He describes finding one such nest complete with eggs.[157]

Unfortunately, frigate birds are known to typically lay only one egg per nesting cycle, leaving us to wonder whether or not the nest described by Pierce was that of another species entirely. Long-time park researcher

Dr. Bill Robertson also questioned the validity of this and other accounts of nesting frigate birds in Florida Bay.[158]

Manatee Key
Charles M. Brookfield had explored the keys of Florida Bay long before they were formally surveyed by the United States. In doing so, he would often mark his charts with informal names to serve as a reference. During the mid-1930's, Brookfield went to work for the U.S. Coast and Geodetic Survey. To assist with their mission of mapping the bay, the surveyors borrowed Brookfield's chart and made copies of it. Much to his surprise, official charts soon appeared bearing his adopted names.

One of these informal names was the moniker for this small island, one of Brookfield's favorite harbors for his 26-foot vessel, *Manatee*.[159]

McLaughlin Key
On a map, this large stretch of land along the Ten Thousand Islands does not appear to be completely surrounded by water. However, in a region where water and land seem to commingle and alternate so readily, there is some latitude to be given to the one who assigned the name "key" to this area.

In truth, it is likely the latter part of the name that was most important to he who coined the term. That honor would be given to John T. McLaughlin, a Lieutenant of the United States Navy during the Second Seminole War. It is fitting that he be recognized in this fashion for two reasons. Firstly, under his command, the United States Navy arguably experienced their greatest success in penetrating the formerly unknown expanse of the Everglades during the Seminole Wars. More importantly, Lieutenant McLaughlin succeeded in producing fairly accurate charts of the labyrinth of rivers and mangrove islands that permeate the West coast. On a trip to Washington in 1841, he boldly asserted that with a sufficient contingent of men, he could navigate to any desired spot in the 'Glades.[160]

Middle Cape Campsite
Three sandy points adorn the southwestern coast of the Cape Sable land mass. Each is named for its geographic location relative to each other. As the name implies, this point lies in the middle between Northwest Cape and East Cape.

Middle Cape Canal
This man-made waterway is named for its proximity to Middle Cape, though its continued existence lies in question. *See also East Cape Canal.*

Middle Fox Lake
This body of water lies in the middle of the chain of Fox Lakes. *See also East Fox Lake.*

Middle Ground
An entry in the Oxford English Dictionary defines "middle ground" as "a shallow place, as a bank or bar."[161] The definition is applicable here, as this moniker is used to designate a shoal area southwest of Flamingo. It is interesting to note that a similar area of shallows is also given this name at the Dry Tortugas, perhaps illustrating its common use in the nautical vernacular.

Middle Lake
During Charles Brookfield's first journey to Seven Palm Lake, he crossed Terrapin Bay and entered McCormick Creek to Monroe Lake. Crossing Monroe Lake, he entered Oyster Creek and reached an unnamed second lake. Because this body of water lay between Monroe Lake and Seven Palm Lake, the location was dubbed Middle Lake.[162]

Monroe Lake
This names seems to have been corrupted somewhat over time. Charles Brookfield states he happened upon this body of water on his first attempt to reach Seven Palm Lake. He further stated that the previously unnamed lake would subsequently be "named Lake Munroe for Wirth Munroe who was on a cruise later with us."[163]

Mormon Key Campsite

It has been suggested that this key is named for early settler Richard Hamilton and his unique "arrangement". Hamilton married a woman in Arcadia, Florida, with whom he fathered four sons and a daughter. Leaving them behind, he later moved to Everglades City where he soon married a second time. This union bore six more children and, in 1895 the family settled on a key at the mouth of the Chatham River. This island would later be known as Mormon Key since it was where Hamilton lived with one of his two living wives.[164] *See also Hog Key Campsite.*

Mosquito Point

It is interesting to note that 42 different species of mosquito have been recorded in Everglades National Park. While most are not blood-suckers (and males do not practice vampirism), that serves as little consolation to those who visit the 'Glades during our summer season. During this time of year, one cannot walk any measurable distance without suffering an assault from a swarm of these trying pests. And, as each individual species actively feeds at different times throughout the day, there is seldom a minute of relief to be had.

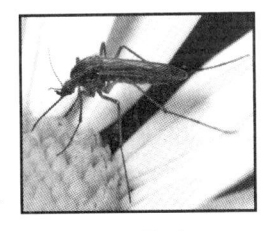

It is truly curious why this particular spit of land would earn the distinction of its current moniker. While the salt marsh mosquitoes that inhabit the mangrove coast are widely regarded to be the most aggressive among their brethren, they are found in abundance along the entire length of the shoreline. The mosquito situation in Flamingo, for example, prompted one person to say that, "one could make a swing with a pint cup and catch a quart of mosquitoes."[165]

While it may never be known why this particular area bears the name Mosquito Point, I doubt any visitors to the area would argue the title.

Mrazek Pond

Named for Vincent J. Mrazek, park ranger at Coot Bay Pond, and later a park naturalist for five years at Flamingo between 1962 and 1967. This pond was formerly known as Barney's Pond for Barney Parker, the first ranger at Everglades National Park.[166]

Mud Bay

Given the amount of detritus that builds beneath every mangrove shoreline, it's a wonder this is the only bay so christened. The true origins of the moniker remain a mystery, though an explanation can be reasonably surmised.

Mud Lake, Mud Lake Canoe Trail

Herbert K. Job, in relaying a trip around 1903 to the mangrove wilderness of Cape Sable, noted, "In the embraces of this swamp lie a series of shallow lakes with muddy bottoms, connected by various channels through the thickets, and more or less overflowed by the sea, especially when strong on-shore winds heap up the waters into the shallow bays." He proceeds to describe an inland journey, writing, "The first lake we visited after an arduous tramp over mangrove roots and through the jungle was a mile long, with densely wooded shores, a mere layer of water over a bed of mud of the consistency of molasses."[167]

In all probability, the lake of which Job writes is not Mud Lake, but his description can be applied to nearly all the lakes in the Cape Sable area. Mangroves drop a considerable quantity of leaves, forming a sizable pile of detritus just below the water's surface. With the passage of time, the decomposition of this organic matter in an anaerobic environment forms a thick layer of nutrient-rich mud. This relatively thick "sludge" can extend several feet in depth, making a walk among the mangroves nearly impossible!

Still, some have asserted the superlative quantity of mud in this body of water. It has been said (with a hint of sarcasm) that those who run Mud Lake with a boat can turn around and light the methane that comes up behind them![168]

The roughly 7-mile long trail circumnavigates the Buttonwood Canal, Coot Bay, Mud Lake, and the Homestead Canal.

Mullet Bay

Four species of mullet commonly inhabit the waters of Everglades National Park. Though primarily found in estuarine habitat, some species are capable of migrating far into freshwater environments.[169]

Though mullet are often pursued as bait, the striped mullet, *Mugil cephalus*, is nonetheless regarded as a food fish of excellent quality.[170]

For settlers in the remote Ten Thousand Islands, mullet provided a plentiful dietary staple.[171] They were a plentiful source of bait for trapping raccoons, whose pelts fetched a decent price in the fur trade.[172] Mullet constituted the primary commercial catch of the area and were frequently salted, dried, and shipped to Cuba and Key West.[173]

Murray Key
Records on this moniker are scarce. Oral accounts tell of a large family by the same name that may have dwelled on the key for a time.[174]

Nest Keys
This island was named for a rather distinctive feature, a tall tree with a prominent osprey nest at the top which could be seen from a long way off, and served as one of the few identifiable landmarks of the otherwise monotonous coastline.[175]

New Turkey Key Campsite
No evidence exists to help explain the basis for this island's current name except that it is near Turkey Key.

Nine Mile Pond, Nine Mile Pond Canoe Trail
In actuality, the trail found at "Nine Mile Pond" is only 5.2 miles long! While a bit confusing to some visitors, the moniker for this pond actually relates to its proximity from the fishing village of Flamingo, nine miles to the south!

Ninemile Bank
This area of shallows is approximately nine miles across at its widest. However, it also lies roughly nine miles from the Keys, leaving the exact origins of its moniker a bit of a mystery.[176]

Noble Hammock Canoe Trail
This waterway is named for Bill Nobles, proprietor of a grocery store in the nearby town of Homestead during the 1920s. Nobles moonlighted in the vicinity of the present-day trail, running a whiskey still in the hammock during Prohibition.[177]

North Harney River
This waterway runs directly north of the Harney River prior to merging with it near the coast. *See also Harney River.*

North Nest Key Campsite
This campsite graces the sand beach of the northern Nest Key. *See also Nest Keys.*

North Plover Key
This island lies to the north of a key by the same name. *See also Plover Key.*

North River, North River Chickee
It has been asserted that this waterway is so named because it does, in fact, lead north out of Whitewater Bay.[178] It should be noted, however, that several nearby channels, including the Watson and Roberts Rivers, do so as well. Why this particular river bears the distinction remains an enigma.

Northwest Cape Campsite
Three sandy points adorn the southwestern coast of the Cape Sable land mass. Each is named for its geographic location relative to each other. As the name implies, this point lies furthest Northwest of the three.

Old Ingraham Campsite, Old Ingraham Highway Trail
This bare-bones campsite is located at the tail end of the Old Ingraham Highway Trail. The roadway is named for James E. Ingraham. The term "old" signifies that this roadway is no longer used by vehicular traffic. It was bypassed in favor of the current main park road in 1956. The biking and hiking Trail on the old roadway is 11.5 miles long. *See also Ingraham Highway.*

Onion Key
Two different stories exist to explain why this small shell island has been so christened. One version tells of an unidentified man who sought refuge in the seclusion and isolation of this area. He homesteaded this island with his wife and cleared a portion of the land to grow onions.[179]

A different version credits Chokoloskee resident Gregorio Lopez with the name, who claimed to have eaten his last onion on the shell island that is now known by this name.[180] The veracity of either story is difficult to gauge, and its entirely possible that both hold some sort of credence.

Opossum Key
The Virginia opossum, *Didelphis virginiana*, is a ubiquitous resident throughout South Florida and bears the unique distinction of being the only marsupial found in North America. This mammal is an opportunistic feeder capable of making a meal of insects, fruit, small vertebrates, garbage and carrion.[181] This widely adaptable nature allows opossums to thrive in most any environment in the sunshine state, from rugged wilderness to urban backyards. Owing largely to their resemblance to a large rat (and often less-than-pleasant attitude), their presence is frowned upon by most and individuals are routinely killed.

This island seems to have earned its name from an overabundance of this animal on the island. Arthur Leslie Darwin, the island's longest-known resident, reported killing great numbers of them during his occupation.[182] *See also Darwin's Place Campsite.*

Otter Creek
It is possible this waterway was named for a profusion of otters found here.

Otter Key
The river otter, *Lutra canadensis*, is a commonly recognized resident in the freshwater interior of the Everglades. This adaptable creature, however, is equally at home in the brackish water of the South Florida coast. Despite their secretive nature, these social carnivores can occasionally be found frolicking together among the tangled roots of mangroves in search of their next meal. Every facet of their anatomy has been perfectly adapted for a life in the water.[183]

Given their aquatic skills and the proximity of this island to the shores of Rankin Bight, it is plausible that otters would at one point both inhabit this key and lend it their name.

Oxfoot Bank
Only a handful of entries have caused the author to throw his hands up in frustration and utter puzzlement. This shallow area in western Florida Bay represents one such entry. In fact, the author personally blames Oxfoot Bank for his receding hairline, as he has torn out clumps at a time in search of an explanation. Unfortunately, no records have been located to explain the origins of this unusual name, and the author now resembles Ron Howard.

Oyster Bay (Cape Sable), Oyster Bay Chickee
Two bays in Everglades National Park share this name. It seems fitting that this particular bivalve receive such recognition, since it figured prominently in the cultural and economic history of the region.

Oysters have been known to grow in great clusters among the mangrove roots of the coast. One account describes them as "hanging several feet above the water" at low tide in "bunches weighing fifty or more pounds each."[184] The harvesting of oyster beds provided a common livelihood for scores of coastal dwellers. While much has been written about the rise of this profitable industry in Florida,[185] it is interesting to note that people have been harvesting these mollusks for thousands of years. Excavations of prehistoric shell mounds throughout South Florida have yielded extensive evidence to suggest the oyster was an important food staple for our indigenous tribes.

Oyster Bay (Ten Thousand Islands)
This bay was likely a prosperous place to collect the shellfish for which it is named.

Oyster Keys
These islands no doubt earned their name from a profusion of bivalves found there at one time.

Pa-hay-okee Overlook Trail
Pa-hay-okee is a word derived from the Hitchiti language of the Seminoles.[186] When translated literally, the term means "grassy water", and provides a fitting description of the expansive Everglades.[187]

Palm Key
Only eight species of palm are native to South Florida, and most may be found close to the coast.[188] A ninth species, the coconut palm, was widely introduced in the area as a plantation crop, and has become one of the area's most ubiquitous species. It is currently unclear which type of palm may have given rise to this island's moniker.

Panhandle Key
Again, from an aerial survey, Brookfield reports this key got its name for its shape.[189]

Park Key
Brookfield recalled that traversing this island by foot was quite easy. With a natural canopy of large black mangrove trees and ground cover of "pickle weed" (Samphire) the island had a park-like quality to it. Hence the key's current moniker.[190] *See also Samphire Key.*

Pass Key
This island was named for the natural channel, or pass, that runs through a shallow bank near its south end.[191]

Paurotis Pond
Eight species of palm occur naturally in Everglades National Park.[192] The Paurotis palm, *Acoelorrhaphe wrightii*, is also referred to as the Everglades palm. It is a fitting name, as it is only found in the United States along the range of the historic Everglades.[193]

This handsome tree can grow to heights of 50 feet or more and is easily identified by its "clumping" growth habit. Large clusters of these trees can be found growing prominently at this stop along the main park road and lend the area their name.

Pavilion Key Campsite

The origins of this moniker take us back nearly two hundred years, to a time when nefarious criminals prowled the coasts of Florida in search of unsuspecting merchant ships. Ironically, one of the most ruthless of these is also one of the least known – a pirate by the name of Charles Gibbs.

Through an act of mutiny, Gibbs assumed command of the *Maria*, a one-time Columbian privateer that would eventually come to fly the black flag. His ruthless crew of brigands did not discriminate among their victims – all cargo was taken, entire crews were murdered, and plundered ships were eventually torched.

Such was the fate of a Dutch merchant ship in 1818. The valuable cargo of West Indian products and silver was promptly plundered and the crew of thirty were massacred – with one exception. A buxom, seventeen-year-old girl, the daughter of a wealthy island planter, was among the crew to be slaughtered. The blond virgin begged mercy of Gibbs. Less from compassion than from his own lust for the girl, he offered a bargain to spare her life. With her consent, the captain brought her to the ship's "rest camp" on an island south of Cape Romano – against the muttering of a reluctant crew.

On the island, Gibbs constructed a pavilion of logs and thatched palm fronds to imprison the girl. The crew held the girl as an anathema, as her testimony would spell certain death in any court of law. Facing a nearly mutinous crew, Gibbs was forced to surrender the girl's life to a council of war, where it was decided that her death would bring the greatest good to the crew of the *Maria*.

Gibbs, unable to bring himself to spill the girl's blood, ordered the ship's cook to poison the girl's meal. After suffering an agonizing death, her body was interred on the island in an unmarked grave.

Not long after the departure of the *Maria*, the United States schooner, *Porpoise*, happened upon this unnamed island on which they found the girl's fresh grave and the pavilion that sheltered her during her final days. Based upon their findings, the ship's Lieutenant penciled in the island's present-day moniker on his charts.

Gibbs would go on to plunder only a short while longer before his reign was put to an abrupt end. Convicted on a count of murder, Gibbs would eventually see his life end at the gallows. He was hanged in New York in April of 1823 at the ripe old age of twenty-nine.[194]

Pearl Bay Chickee

One source suggests that this bay was traditionally known as an area where Indians found oysters containing pearls.[195] Unfortunately, no other corroborating information can be found. True or not, those who have had the pleasure of spending a winter evening on this remote platform have indeed found a valuable treasure.

Pelican Keys

Pelicans are perhaps one of the most easily recognizable birds of the South Florida coast. Throughout the year, brown pelicans can be spotted skimming the waters of Florida Bay and roosting near the shoreline. During the winter months, the area also sees an influx of migrant white pelicans from across the country.

It is not uncommon to find whole forests of these trees painted white with guano – testament to the numbers and frequency with which pelicans gather. It has been suggested that pelicans have previously nested on this key.[196]

Peterson Keys

Formerly known as the Bowlegs Keys, these islands seem to have been renamed to commemorate Roger Torey Peterson, renowned birder and founder of a series of field guides bearing his name.[197] As a prominent member of the National Audubon Society, Peterson would come to work closely with colleague Robert Porter Allen over the course of many years.[198] Starting in 1939, Allen spent two years conducting extensive studies of the roseate spoonbill population on the islands of Florida Bay. In his published findings, Allen acknowledged Peterson's assistance in the lengthy project.[199] Thus, it seems probable that Peterson did visit the area, though evidence linking him to these particular islands is scarce. *See also Buchanan Keys.*

Everglades National Park

Picnic Key Campsite
Though no official documentation exists, it has been said that this area received its name for the fact that locals would often gather there for a big picnic dinner.[200] This represents the best available explanation to date.

Pine Glades Lake
An "ecotone" is a term ecologists use to describe an area of transition between two clearly distinct habitats. It is an appropriate designation for this particular area. The lake lies at the interface of two major ecosystems in park – the "pine" rocklands and the open sawgrass prairie, or, "glade".

Pineland Trail
Many visitors are surprised to find a pine forest in the middle of the Everglades! Yet this upland community thrives atop a rocky ridge that provides a suitable elevation and substrate on which to grow. Also referred to as "pine rockland", this ecosystem is by far the most biologically diverse region in the park.

The short, half-mile trail leads visitors on a walk through a typical South Florida pineland. Here one might be able to find a bounty of wildflowers, butterflies, and birds.

Plate Creek Bay, Plate Creek Bay Chickee
Gregorio Lopez has been credited for christening the creek that feeds this tiny body of water by the same name. As fate would have it, Lopez claimed to have lost a plate while once traversing this previously unnamed waterway.[201]

Plover Key
Seven members of the plover family have been recorded in Everglades National Park.[202] Most are fairly common residents that can be observed along the coast with some regularity. It is unclear, therefore, for which bird this key is named.

Pollock Keys
The origin of this name is unknown.

Ponce de Leon Bay

Spanish explorer Juan Ponce de Leon is frequently credited with discovering the land that he would come to christen "La Florida". Contrary to popular lore, he sailed the coastline in both 1512 and 1521 not in search of a mythical fountain, but for gold. His quest for wealth would ultimately lead him to his death at the hands of hostile Indians.[203]

Before his passing, he left his name upon a vast inlet that would eventually come to be known as Charlotte Harbor. Over the course of centuries, the countless cartographers who labored to best represent the tortuous waterways of the area drew and redrew its lines. From map to map, the coast would undulate and reform itself, while new names would arise to displace the old. Maps show the location of Ponce de Leon Bay today, likely as the result of their constant evolution.

Porjoe Key

It has been written that "porjoe" is a common nickname of the great blue heron in the Caribbean.[204] Because it bears the distinction of being the tallest wading bird in South Florida, it is conceivable that this conspicuous species might serve as the namesake of this mangrove key. Still, it is questionable how such a robust species would ever come to be known by such a moniker.

Others have asserted that this term is applied instead to the Louisiana (or tricolored) heron, in photo left. It has been said that the bird's scrawny, underfed appearance gave birth to the name.[205] It is most likely that this island was christened for the presence of these birds here at one time.

Porpoise Point

The Atlantic bottlenose dolphin is a common resident in the waters of Florida Bay. Over the years, the terms "dolphin" and "porpoise" have often been used interchangeably. Given our current understanding of the difference between the two, however, it would appear that this spit of land has been granted something of a misnomer. Still, being one of the most conspicuous residents along the coast, it is most likely that the area was named for their presence.[206]

Possum Key
See Opossum Key.

Rabbit Keys, Rabbit Key Campsite, Rabbit Keys Basin, Pass

Present-day visitors may find it odd that, while several keys bear this same moniker, rabbits are seldom found off the mainland. It has been noted that at one time, however, many of the outer keys did have rabbits living on them. These were likely the common marsh rabbit, *Sylvilagus palustris*, that are found on the mainland. Since the crushing blows of Hurricane Donna in 1960, however, few of the smaller mammalian species seem to have repopulated these keys.[207]

The Basin is of slightly deeper water west of the keys and the Pass is a natural channel running to the Lopez River.

Rankin Key, Rankin Bight

That so little is known of the African-American experience in the Everglades is truly unfortunate. Yet what little remains seems to indicate that, for most, it was a difficult life. While Mother Nature dealt out her own series of hardships, prevailing societal norms exerted their own influence.

Consider the case of Rankin, a black squatter who lived on this key during Prohibition. He earned a meager living cutting buttonwood and working as a charcoal burner. Prohibition officers, or "prohis" as they were called, patrolled the waters regularly looking for hidden stills and rum runners. Prosecuting a war on liquor often proved difficult in the labyrinth of the Everglades. Success was hard to come by and law enforcement was always eager to make a statement.

On one occasion, a group of "prohis" made a surprise visit to Rankin at his camp. Despite his innocence, they eagerly chopped up his water still and took a series of pictures. The following day, they issued a news release regarding their recent discovery and destruction of a moonshine operation.[208]

Roberts River, Roberts River Chickee

Concrete details regarding the nomenclature of this river are difficult to acquire. It has been suggested that this waterway was named for "Uncle Steve" Roberts, a turn-of-the-century Flamingo resident.[209]

In 1895, Roberts moved from Orlando to the Cape Sable area with his wife, Dora Jane, and his sons, Ward, Eugene, Melch, and Loren.[210] In 1915 Roberts expanded his home to a two-story structure and offered lodging to those visiting the Cape. The Roberts Hotel, as it was known, remained the most conspicuous structure at Flamingo until it was destroyed by a Hurricane in 1926.[211] The Roberts family remained in Flamingo until the establishment of the national park in 1947. *See also Carl Ross Key.*

Rocky Creek Bay

This inland body of water lies at the headwaters of the creek by the same name. Rocky Creek is so christened for the pinnacle rock that can clearly be seen just below the surface in the upper reaches of the creek during low water.[212]

Rodgers River Bay Chickee

It has been suggested that this area may have been named in honor of Colonel St. George Rodgers, who led the Florida Mounted Volunteers on raids in the area in 1857.[213]

Rookery Branch
This waterway is situated at the southern end of the Shark River Slough and becomes one of the headwater streams of the Shark River. It is named for a large bird rookery that could be found on a hammock near its northernmost terminus. At one time, this was regarded as the most prolific rookery in the Everglades, hosting over 1,000,000 birds at a time.[214]

Roscoe Key
Charles Brooksfield recalls an expedition he made with Roscoe Dunton, formerly the first division manager of the Caribbean Division of Pan American Airways. Accompanying the two men were Mr. Dunton's wife Luvenia, his daughter Florence (whose nickname was "Topsy"), Earl Montgomery and Sid Newcomb. The group tried to get Dunton's vessel, *Topsy*, as close to Seven Palm Lake as possible. During the course of the expedition, the group encountered several unnamed keys and gave them monikers commemorating those on board.[215] *See also Sid Key and Topsy Key.*

Rowdy Bend Trail
No documentation currently exists to explain the origins of this curious moniker.

Russell Key
This island is named for the Russell family who maintained a large chicken farm on the island and later moved to Oregon. A large poinciana tree still marks the landing where the Russell home was located in 1890.[216]

Samphire Keys
This key derives its name from the abundance of samphire, *Blutaparon vermiculare*, the sprawling perennial that adorns its shores.[217] The plant flowers year round and may have proven important to settlers for its edibility by both people and livestock.[218]

Sandfly Island

Of all the biting flies that thrive in South Florida, none is perhaps as reviled as the sandfly. Otherwise known as no-see-ums or "punkies", the small insects can often penetrate screening that other insects cannot.[219]

Like mosquitoes, female sandflies require blood to incubate their young, and the quest for this elixir of life causes great annoyance to humans.[220]

The area was a thriving tomato-farming location in the early 1900s, settled by "Uncle Charley" Boggess and others.[221]

Sandy Key

Charles William Pierce, in recounting a five-month expedition through the Florida Keys in 1885, wrote of this island that it "is well named as it is not much more than a sand bank with some beach grass growing on it, and a few mangroves on the inside shore."[222] Dr. William Robertson, a long-time researcher at Everglades National Park, noted that in subsequent years the island supported a more extensive floral community. However, due to the cyclic force of powerful storms in South Florida, it is likely that the island will be stripped clean once again in coming years.

Santini Bight

This bight was named for the pioneering Chokoloskee family of the same name. Long-time Flamingo resident Coleman Irwin seems to have had a hand in the christening of this body of water. Locals of the area had known it previously as Big Island Bight but, upon being asked by a surveyor in the 1930s, Irwin offered its current name. The Santini family was known to travel far and wide around South Florida in the pursuit of game,[223] and Victor Santini fished this location frequently.[224]

Schooner Bank

While it can be assumed that many "schooners" have indeed plied the waters of Florida Bay, no evidence suggests why this particular area should be so christened.

Second Bay
This is the second major bay to be encountered along Lostmans River when being traveled inland from the Gulf. *See also First Bay.*

Seven Palm Lake
This body of water found just east of West Lake and Cuthbert Lake derives its name from the seven stately royal palms which once adorned its banks. These palms grew in such a straight fashion as to have someone believe they were planted there.[225]

Sadly, the shores of the lake are no longer lined with these majestic specimens. All but one died in the aftermath of the Labor Day Hurricane of 1935. The sole survivor would later succumb to the fierce winds of Hurricane Donna in 1960.[226]

Shark Point (Ten Thousand Islands)
This interesting moniker has been granted to two distinct areas in Everglades National Park. One is situated along the shore of Florida Bay, while the other lies a considerable distance away among the Ten Thousand Islands. This occurrence speaks well of the profusion and distribution of sharks within the coastal waters of the park.

Shark River, Shark River Chickee
Following a winter fishing expedition to this waterway, famed author Zane Grey postulated that its name was a misnomer. Not only was the big-game angler disappointed to find no sharks, he also found the passage to be little more than a "winding green creek, with many side channels, making the mangrove forest a matter of many islands".[227]

The complex of mangrove shoreline and warm, coastal waters described by Grey are important nursery grounds for a variety of marine organisms. The thick tangle of mangrove roots that are prevalent in the area provide the ideal shelter for juvenile sea life – including sharks.

While exploring the waters around Cape Sable, Hugh L. Willoughby reported watching "the shark and tarpon that were occasionally rising to the surface."[228] In recent years, such anecdotal observations have been corroborated by systematic research. Bill Loftus, a long-time fisheries biologist for Everglades National Park, confirms a persistent population of bull sharks in this river.[229]

EVERGLADES NATIONAL PARK

Despite Grey's disappointing venture, thirteen varieties of shark have been recorded in the waters of Everglades National Park. Some occur more commonly than others, and it has been noted that bull sharks, black tip sharks, lemon sharks, and bonnetheads are among the more abundant species of the area.[230]

Shark Valley
Visitors would be hard-pressed to find any sharks around this completely land-locked area. However, the real draw here is the Shark River Slough (pronounced "slew"), a landscape feature of lower elevation that funnels water from the north in a southwesterly direction towards the Gulf of Mexico. The majority of this water finds its way to the ocean via several major waterways. One of these is the Shark River, which being an estuary between fresh and salt water, serves as a nursery ground for the bull shark, *Carcharhinus leucas*. Thus the "valley" is named for the river into which it empties.

Shell Key
Entire books have been written about the exploits of shell collectors in South Florida.[231] While shell deposits in the area are localized and not widespread, it is plausible that this island has become known for one of these accumulations.

Sid Key
This island was named by Charles Brookfield for Sid Newcome, a passenger on his ship, the *Manatee*.[232] See also Roscoe Key.

Sisal Pond
Famed botanist Henry Perrine is credited with discovering *Agave sisalana*, a species of hemp plant he would later come to introduce in several locales in South Florida in the early 1840s.[233] The progeny of these horticultural experiments persists to this day and grow in abundance near this pond which bears their name.

Snake Bight, Snake Bight Trail

Given its intimidating name, it's a wonder anyone ventures out on this trail. However, the area is named more for its geography and lore than its actual inhabitants. The term "bight" signifies any bend in the coast forming an open bay. The term may also correctly be applied to the bay formed by such a bend. Such is the case here.

Everglades National Park boasts 28 different varieties of snake, and it is entirely plausible that this area may have proven a favorite haunting ground for any one (or several) of these. Still, serpents can be found in every corner of the park's million-and-a-half acres, leading one to wonder exactly why this spot should earn the distinction over all others.

The answer may lie in the local lore of Flamingo and Florida Bay. Over the years, there have been persistent rumors of exceptionally large snakes inhabiting the area. In recounting his travels through Florida Bay in 1898, Hugh Willoughby remembers the many tales he had heard regarding the presence of large serpents living in the 'Glades. One of his guides, Ed Brewer, took Willoughby to the location where he had killed, over a year prior, what was the largest snake he had ever seen. Given Willoughby's description, it would appear they were in the area of Trout Cove, well east of Flamingo. Here they recovered roughly two-thirds of the remains of a large viper that Willoughby surmised to be an eight-foot long rattlesnake.

While indeed a large specimen, Willoughby's rattlesnake did not "measure up" to reported accounts. He remained convinced of their plausibility writing, "The great snakes of some species do exist in Florida, yet to be discovered, I have not the slightest doubt. I pin my faith to the account that two different Indians have given me of snakes that were at least eighteen feet in length, and evidently belonged to the constrictor family. As I have remarked before, I have never known a Seminole to lie." [234] These same legends remain in circulation even today.[235]

According to long-time Flamingo resident "Uncle Steve" Roberts, these legends were fact.[236] Still, it has also been suggested that this moniker came about from the odd sense of humor shared by those that lived in the area of Cape Sable.

The Trail is 1.5 miles to the coast and the small jetty at the end overlooking the Bight affords some of the best birding in the park.

EVERGLADES NATIONAL PARK

Snake Key
It is interesting to note that all snakes can swim. While some are naturally more aquatic than others, each is capable of staying afloat and undulating to varying degrees of effectiveness. Their impermeable, reptilian skin also allows them to manage quite well when introduced into salt water.

Still, few snakes from the freshwater interior of the 'Glades ever venture to coastal areas like those where this island resides. There is, however, one notable exception. The diamondback rattlesnake, *Croatalus adamanteus*, has been known to occasionally migrate between mangrove islands over saltwater.[237] This large, well-known species is easily recognized and may account for the island's current moniker.

However, it should be noted that there are a handful of snakes that do regularly inhabit the coast. The most common of these is the mangrove salt marsh snake, *Nerodia clarkii compressicauda*.[238] It is also plausible that this island may have been named for an abundance of this snake.

South Joe River Chickee
This camping platform lies near the southern terminus of Joe River. *See also Joe River.*

Spy Key
This island was named by the crew of the United States Coast and Geodetic Survey Schooner *Spy* for their ship, which was used in the first hydrographic survey of the area in 1890.[239]

Stake Key
Historically, stakes and pipes were commonly used as navigational aids in the treacherous shallow waters of coastal South Florida. Despite great advancements in marking high-traffic areas with formal, highly visible markers, boaters in the area still happen upon numerous examples of worn PVC or wooden markers intended to provide cryptic guidance between lesser-known locations. It is plausible that some such arrangement may have given rise to this island's current moniker.

Storter Bay

This bay at the mouth of the Huston and Chatham Rivers is named for the Storter family who settled in what is now Everglades City in the 1880s. George Storter, Jr., built the farm that would later serve as a boarding house for travelers and sportsmen. He was the postmaster and operated a trading post that was frequented by both whites and Indians. His brother Bembery shipped local produce to Key West and carried the mail.[240] Bembery's son Rob wrote about their experiences in *Crackers in the Glade* which is illustrated with his charming sketches.[241]

The Storters would eventually become the progenitors of a large West Coast family.[242] George's historic home was bought by Barron Collier and exists to this day, though it is known in its current incarnation as The Rod and Gun Lodge.[243]

Sunday Bay, Sunday Bay Chickee

No viable explanation has yet been found to explain the origins of this moniker.

Swash Keys

The origins of this island's name currently remains a mystery.

Sweet Bay Pond

This pond is named for the sweet bay tree, *Magnolia virginiana*, which is commonly abundant throughout the Everglades. Old timers in the area would use this tree to make a sort of tea, stripping the tender young leaves and bringing them to a boil.[244]

Sweetwater Bay Chickee

This campsite, and the bay in which it is situated, no doubt derive their current monikers from a stream nearby of the same name. Freshwater would pulse down this river during the rainy season, giving it the name Sweet Water. It served as an important source of drinking water for the recent inhabitants of the area, and was likely crucial to the Indian cultures that built shell mounds on nearby Opossum Key.[245]

Everglades National Park

Tarpon Bay

One of the fish most eagerly sought by anglers in South Florida waters is the tarpon. While this species is edible, it is the sport of bringing one in that proves most exciting. The fever to snare one of these immense, "silver kings" permeates the coastal communities of the area annually.

Charles Richard Dodge, on a trip from Tampa to Cape Sable in the 1890s, reported that along the coast, "there is but one topic of conversation in the fishing season – the tarpon." Dodge goes on to hint at the allure of tarpon fishing, "Fancy playing for two hours at the end of a slender bass line, over thirty fathoms long, a gamey fish weighing one hundred and fifty pounds, and some idea will be formed of the skill required to keep the fish on the line, or the line from parting, and the excitement attending the final capture."[246]

It is plausible that this inland bay was at one time ripe with tarpon, especially given its geography. This bay is fed by the Shark River and remains a popular locale for pursuing the popular game fish for which it is named.

Tarpon Creek

It is likely that tarpon can frequently be encountered in this narrow waterway.

Taylor Slough

This slough is named for its southern drainage, the Taylor River. The river, in turn, is most likely named for President Zachary Taylor (1784-1850). Following his victory in the Battle of Okeechobee during the Seminole Wars, General Taylor received chief command of Florida in 1838.[247] Commemorating his extensive service, his surname has christened creeks, rivers and counties of the sunshine state.

That President Taylor serves as the namesake for this watershed represents the author's best educated guess. Unfortunately, no documentation has been found to directly link the individual with this feature. Furthermore, the name of "Taylor's River" first appears on the United States Geologic Survey map of Florida in 1909 – over half a decade after President Taylor's demise.

While the river has borne the name Taylor for quite some time, it is interesting to note that the slough has not. It has been asserted that the current moniker was first used following the creation of the national park in 1947. Prior to the building of roads and bridges in the area, pioneers forged the slough by foot. Old timers of the area often waded through the hip deep water which, during cooler weather, consistently yielded the same result. Consequently dubbed "Deadpecker Slough", this former name was dropped by the National Park Service and christened something a bit less prurient.[248]

Ten Thousand Islands
Although it is doubtful that anyone has actually counted the islands, the winding labyrinth of mangroves, keys and waterways can certainly lead a mariner to believe that so many do exist.

Zane Grey, in recounting a lengthy fishing trip through the area, once wrote, "It seemed I had seen all the Ten Thousand Islands of the region. The error was not in the number I had seen, but in the name. It should have been designated by a hundred thousand instead of ten."[249]

Tern Keys
There are 11 species of terns that have been observed in Everglades National Park. Of these, four are commonly seen.[250] Most terns utilize similar habitats for nesting, and several species are often found together.

This island was specifically named for a nesting colony of least terns (photo right) that was once found there.[251] The least tern is our most diminutive species and is now classified as a Federally protected endangered species.

Terrapin Bay

Three distinct subspecies of diamondback terrapin, *Malaclemmys terrapin ssp.*, have been identified in Everglades National Park.[252] Their unique skin pattern, consisting of dark spotting against a light gray ground color, renders these medium-sized turtles easy to identify. These hearty reptiles thrive in the salty waters of the coast and are adapted for a life in saline water. Special glands near the eyes allow the animal to secrete excess salt.[253]

It is entirely plausible that great populations of these turtles thrived in and around the bay that bears their name. Historically, terrapins were abundant in most lagoons and shallows along the Florida coast, though today they appear far more scarce. It has been suggested that continued harvesting for their edible meat and eggs, as well as wide-spread habitat loss, has been responsible for their decline.

Terrapin Point

This spit of land is one of three locations to be named for the salt-water diamond-back terrapins that call these coastlines home. *See also Dead Terrapin Key.*

The Cutoff

In the 1817 publication *A Dictionary of American English on Historical Principles*, the term "cut-off" was defined as being used to denote a sluggish stream that connected two rivers.[254] This description certainly applies here, as this narrow waterway serves as a bridge between Roberts River and North River.

The Lungs

While others have mentioned the unique shape of this body of water,[255] the credit for christening this area goes to Roscoe Dunton and Charles Brookfield. The pair chartered the Goodyear blimp to survey the area for a possible route to enter Seven Palm Lake. While looking down from above, they noticed an unusual feature on the landscape – a pair of connected lakes that resembled a large pair of lungs. And so it has been known ever since![256]

Everglades National Park

Third Bay
This is the third major bay to be encountered along Lostmans River when being traveled inland from the Gulf. *See also First Bay.*

Tiger Key Campsite
That the name "Tiger" is popular in the Seminole and Miccosukee culture is probably indicative that the origins of this moniker are likely related to Native Americans in the area. However, no documentation specifies which individual this name is meant to honor.

Topsy Key
This island is named for Florence Dunton.[257] *See also Roscoe Key.*

Triplet Keys
This apparent "little group of three" was named as such by Charles Brooksfield.[258]

Trout Cove
It has been noted that in the past, Florida's ubiquitous largemouth bass were often referred to as trout.[259] It is unlikely, however, that these popular freshwater sport fish would have been found in the brackish bay that bears this name.

However, two species of sea trout, *Cynoscion nebulosis* and *Cynoscion arenarius*, are known to inhabit the waters of Everglades National Park.[260] While no "official" explanation exists, it is likely that this sheltered bay was named for an abundance of these tasty fish.

Turkey Key Campsite
It is plausible that this island may have been name for a colony of anhingas that may have existed here at one time. These birds are often known locally as "water turkeys" due to their aquatic nature, broad tails and distinct coloration. *See also Anhinga Trail.*

Everglades National Park

Turner River
This waterway was named for Captain Richard Bushrod Turner[261] who served as a guide for Florida's volunteer forces during the Third Seminole War.[262] He would later become one of the first white settlers of the area, homesteading on a large shell mound near the headwaters of the river that bears his name.[263] *See also Turner River Canoe Trail in Big Cypress National Preserve.*

Turtle Key
Five different species of sea turtle inhabit the waters of South Florida. These include the leatherback, Kemps ridley, Atlantic hawksbill, green and loggerhead. By far, the loggerhead, *Caretta caretta*, is most common, often utilizing area beaches for nesting during the summer season. It is most probable that this island is named for their presence.

Twin Keys, Twin Keys Bank
While no official record exists, one can easily surmise that these islands derived their name from their close proximity and resemblance of appearance. A natural channel separates the two. The Bank lies just west of the keys.

Two Island Bay
This bay is named for the pair of islands that are located within.

Umbrella Key
This island was formerly adorned by a large mangrove that grew in the shape of an umbrella. This particular tree was quite conspicuous on the horizon and served as an important navigational aid for local fishermen.[264]

Upper Arsnicker Keys
Of the group of "Arsnicker" keys in the park, these are situated farthest north. *See also Arsenicker Key in Biscayne National Park.*

Watson Place Campsite

This campsite sits on the grounds of the former home site of Edward J. Watson. Perhaps no other drama of the Everglades backcountry has been as well chronicled as that of "Bloody Ed". During the 1890s, Watson homesteaded a large parcel of land near the mouth of the Chatham River. He proved a very successful farmer, growing sugarcane and vegetables for the Key West market. So successful were his ventures, he was able to construct what was undoubtedly one of the finest homes in the Ten Thousand Islands, and visitors to the campsite can still find the concrete pillars to this two story structure.

Shortly following his arrival in the 1890s Watson developed a reputation as something of a shady character. Those that knew him well were privy to stories from his past, wherein he recalled relations with notorious outlaws and admitted to killing no fewer than four victims.[265]

For the most part, Watson proved neighborly to most residents in the area[266] but a string of violent and unexplained occurrences soon gave way to greater suspicion. During an altercation at a Key West auction house, Watson slashed the throat of Adolphus Santini. While Santini survived the attack, the incident cost Watson bitterly to settle. Around this time Watson's former wife, whom he had deserted in Oregon, learned of his whereabouts. "Bloody Ed" arranged to have her move down with him, only to have her die under suspicious circumstances.

Over the next few years, several victims found murdered in the area had had dealings with Watson, and popular opinion blamed him as the cause. Needless to say, rumors circulated with a fury and locals began to avoid the Watson residence at all cost.

A little farther down river from his home, Watson maintained a separate building for boat storage and quarters for laborers. Much has been surmised about the composition of his work force. Watson employed numerous people, some of whom were friends and neighbors, while the balance were often vagabonds, drifters, or those seeking asylum from the law. For these, Watson offered work with no questions asked. Given his apparent success in business, it has been suggested that

Watson profited from the labor of those for whom he arranged an early "retirement".[267]

In 1910, one such motley crew arrived seeking work from Watson. Not long after, a neighbor named Cannon *(see Cannon Bay)* found the murdered body of one of the laborers in the shallow waters of Chatham River. Nearby residents were quickly alerted and it was later learned, from one who escaped the massacre, that no fewer than four others had been slain. Watson was quick to accuse one of his employees for the murders, but community opinion ran contrary. During a confrontation outside the Smallwood Store in Chokoloskee, Watson became enraged at the group that had gathered to accuse him of homicide. He pulled a shotgun on the crowd and pulled the trigger, but the wet shells in his firearm failed him. The reign of "Bloody Ed" Watson quickly ended as he was mowed down in a hail of bullets.[268]

Not long after his demise, numerous accounts circulated about the location of human remains at the Watson place. Dozens of skeletons were reported to have been found interred around the grounds of the homestead.[269]. The veracity of these claims will perhaps never be known. The story was fictionalized by Peter Matthiessen in *Killing Mister Watson*, a popular novel about the area and the event.

Visitors today will find only the remains of his sugar cane plantation, including the kettle used to boil his syrup.

Watson River, Watson River Chickee

Sport fishing became increasingly popular in the area of Flamingo during the 1930s. Cashing in on the trend, an entrepreneur named Louis Watson started a charter boat business out of Coot Bay Pond around this time. Watson's Fish Camp was the point of origin for numerous fishing expeditions into the backcountry.[270]

In order to facilitate the passage between the two bodies of water, Captain Watson dredged a channel connecting Coot Bay to Coot Bay Pond in 1945.[271] The waterway exists today and affords travelers access to the many creeks and rivers around Whitewater Bay, including the one that today bears Watson's name.[272] *See also Coot Bay Pond.*

The camping platform lies just southeast of the mouth of the Watson River.

West Key
While no official documentation exist to corroborate this claim, it is most likely that this island was named for its position in relation to the coastline of the Florida Keys.

West Lake, West Lake Canoe Trail, West Lake Trail
This is the westernmost body of water one encounters in traversing the chain of lakes beyond Alligator Creek. It is also the largest, providing ample opportunity for a variety of recreational options to visitors.

The 7.5 mile canoe trail crosses the expanse of West Lake before winding through a chain of smaller lakes on the way to Alligator Creek.

The short, quarter-mile boardwalk leads visitors through a tangled mangrove forest that eventually opens to a serene view of West Lake.

Whaleback Key
This mangrove key was named during a survey of Florida Bay in the 1930's. Lt. Matheson, who was charged with charting the area, thought the island resembled the back of a whale from a distance.[273]

Whipray Basin, Whipray Keys
Jacob R. Motte served as an army surgeon during the Second Seminole War. His written memoirs provide a telling account of South Florida during the late 1830s. During an exploring expedition among the southerly keys, he writes "In returning to shore, or rather to the rock, the Colonel amused himself in harpooning the denizens of these waters, through whose clear depths they could be distinctly perceived, slowly moving about. Among others he succeeded in securing an immense *Sting-ray* and *Whip-ray*, the latter so called from the length and appearance of its tail."[274]

These creatures seem to have been plentiful in the area even through the twentieth century, as one can find numerous mention of their presence. Park biologist Joseph Curtis Moore recounts the character of the area that may have given rise to its current name. "The banks of Whipray Channel", writes Moore, "were steep and somewhat undercut where it narrowly separated two of the Whipray Keys. From the deep shadow under the bank into the crystal clear water beneath us ... a kite-like Whipray glided near the bottom beneath us and on out of sight."[275]

Former residents of the area also report much success in catching great quantities of whiprays and stingrays in the vicinity of the channel that bears this name. They were sought after as a plentiful bait for stone crab traps.[276]

Whitewater Bay

Winds often play upon this large expanse of water, leaving the bay choppy and covered with white caps.[277] Such hazards to navigation no doubt gave rise the area's current moniker. What is most interesting is that this name may have originated from the Seminole language.

Linguist William A. Read asserts that the term "whitewater" is a translation of the Seminole name *wiwahàtki, wiwa* meaning "water" and *hàtki* meaning "white". Read notes that the latter phrase was also used to refer to the ocean, and further serves to illustrate the bay's similarity to open water.[278]

Willy Willy Campsite

This area once served as the campsite for a Seminole by the same name. Willy Willy was easily recognized by virtue of a conspicuous cropped ear. It is widely believed that he was a tribal outcast, who suffered this injury at the hands of his people as a form of retribution for some wrong committed. He was known to whites as a smuggler who hunted egret plumes around 1910 after such activity was illegal.[279]

Wood Key

Much has been written about the extensive stands of useful lumber that grew in abundance along the South Florida coast.[280] It is likely that this island was named for an abundance of one (or several) of these species.

EVERGLADES NATIONAL PARK

Wood River

It seems no definitive evidence exists to suggest why this waterway would be so christened. It is plausible that, at one time, an abundance of commercially important lumber might have been found here. The true question, however, is which of these species was harvested. West Indian mahogany, black mangrove and buttonwood are all coastal species that were harvested for a variety of reasons. Any or all of these may have given rise to the river's current moniker.

REFERENCES

[1] Douglas, Marjory Stoneman. *The Everglades: River of Grass*. Pineapple Press. Sarasota, FL. 1947. Reprint 1997. Pg. 7.

[2] Robertson, William B., Jr. *Everglades: The Park Story*. Florida National Parks and Monuments Association. Miami, FL. 1989.

[3] Woolfenden, Glen. E. "In memoriam: William B. Robertson, Jr., 1924-2000". *The Auk*. July, 2001.

[4] Tebeau, Charlton W. *Man in the Everglades*. University of Miami Press. Miami, FL. 1968. Pg. 179.

[5] Douglas, Marjory Stoneman. *The Everglades: River of Grass*. Pineapple Press. Sarasota, FL. 1947. Reprint 1997.

[6] Brookfield, Charles M. & Oliver Griswold. *They All Called it Tropical*. Historical Association of Southern Florida. Miami, FL. 1949.

[7] Brown, William E. & Karen Hudson. *Model Land Company Records*. University of Miami. Coral Gables, FL. June 1993.

[8] Tebeau, Charlton W. *Man in the Everglades*. University of Miami Press. Miami, FL. 1968. Pg. 172.

[9] McIver, Stuart. *True Tales of the Everglades*. Florida Flair Books. 1989. Pg. 9.

[10] Douglas, Marjory Stoneman. *Voice of the River, an Autobiography*. Pineapple Press, Sarasota, FL. 1987.

[11] Burt, Al. *Becalmed in the Mullet Latitudes*. Miami Herald Publishing Company. Miami, FL. 1983. Pg. 132.

[12] Tebeau, Charlton W. *Man in the Everglades*. University of Miami Press. Miami, FL. 1968. Pgs. 172-173.

[13] Brown, Loren G. "Totch". *Totch: A Life in the Everglades*. University Press of Florida. Gainesville, FL. 1993. Pg. 36.

[14] Simmons, Glen & Laura Ogden. *Gladesmen: Gator Hunters, Moonshiners, and Skiffers*. University Press of Florida. Gainesville, FL. 1998. Pg. 72.

[15] Simmons, Glen & Laura Ogden. *Gladesmen: Gator Hunters, Moonshiners, and Skiffers*. University Press of Florida. Gainesville, FL. 1998. Pg. 174.

[16] Dilley, Willard E. "Our Three Bears". *Everglades Natural History*. Everglades Natural History Association. December 1954. Vol. 2 No. 4. Pg. 189-192.

[17] Maxwell, Ralph. Interview, 1968. *Everglades Place Names Card File* Everglades National Park Archives.

[18] Dilley, Willard E. "Our Three Bears". *Everglades Natural History*. Everglades Natural History Association. December 1954. Vol. 2 No. 4. Pg. 189-192.

[19] Brookfield, Charles Mann. Interview by Love Dean. Early 1982. Islamorada Branch, Monroe Public Library. Later printed as an article for *Florida Keys Magazine*, First Quarter, 1982.

[20] Andrews, Allen H. *A Yank Pioneer in Florida*. Douglas Printing Co., Inc. Jacksonville, FL. 1950. Pg. 268.

[21] Beard, Daniel B. *Everglades National Park Project*. National Park Service. United States Department of the Interior. 1938. Pg. 39.

[22] *Everglades Place Names Card File*. Everglades National Park Archives. 1958-1985.

[23] Murphy, Larry E., Editor. *Dry Tortugas National Park Submerged Cultural Resources Assessment*. National Park Service. Santa Fe, New Mexico. 1993. Pg. 57.

[24] Zollo, Cathy. "Deep Trouble: Black Tide". *Naples Daily News*. October 9, 2003.

[25] Allen, Robert P. *Flame Birds*. Dodd, Mead & Co, New York, NY. 1942.

[26] Sprunt IV, Alexander. "In Memoriam: Robert Porter Allen". *The Auk*. January, 1969. Vol. 86, 26-34.

[27] Willoughby, Hugh L. *Across the Everglades*. Florida Classics Library. Port Selerno, FL. 1898. Pg. 83.

[28] Brookfield, Charles Mann. Interview by Love Dean. Early 1982. Islamorada Branch, Monroe Public Library. Later printed as an article for *Florida Keys Magazine*, First Quarter, 1982.

[29] Brookfield, Charles Mann. Interview by Love Dean. Early 1982. Islamorada Branch, Monroe Public Library. Later printed as an article for *Florida Keys Magazine*, First Quarter, 1982.

[30] Tebeau, Charlton W. *Man in the Everglades*. University of Miami Press. Miami, FL. 1968. Pg. 146.

[31] McIver, Stuart B. *Death in the Everglades: The Murder of Guy Bradley, America's First Martyr to Environmentalism*. University Press of Florida. Gainesville, FL. 2003.

[32] Miele, Ralph. *Everglades Place Names Card File*. Everglades National Park Archives. 1958-1985.

[33] Davison, Ann. *Florida Junket*. Peter Davies, Ltd. London, England. 1964. Pg. 83.

[34] Brookfield, Charles Mann. Interview by Love Dean. Early 1982. Islamorada Branch, Monroe Public Library. Later printed as an article for *Florida Keys Magazine*, First Quarter, 1982.

[35] Brookfield, Charles Mann. Interview by Love Dean. Early 1982. Islamorada Branch, Monroe Public Library. Later printed as an article for *Florida Keys Magazine*, First Quarter, 1982.

[36] *Everglades Place Names Card File*. Everglades National Park Archives. 1958-1985.

[37] Ross, Carl. Interview, 1968. *Everglades Place Names Card File*. Everglades National Park Archives. 1958-1985.

[38] Maxwell, Ralph. Interview, 1968. *Everglades Place Names Card File*. Everglades National Park Archives. 1958-1985.

[39] Will, Lawrence E. *A Dredgeman of Cape Sable*. The Glades Historical Society. Belle Glade, FL. 1968. Pg. 69.

[40] Sibley, David Allen. *The Sibley Guide to Birds*. Alfred A. Knopf. New York. 2000. Pg. 107.

[41] Brookfield, Charles Mann. Interview by Love Dean. Early 1982. Islamorada Branch, Monroe Public Library. Later printed as an article for *Florida Keys Magazine*, First Quarter, 1982.

[42] Paige, John C. *Historic Resource Study for Everglades National Park*. National Park Service. 1986.

[43] Tebeau, Charlton W. *Man in the Everglades*. University of Miami Press. Miami, FL. 1968. Pg. 42.

[44] Maxwell, Ralph. Interview, 1968. *Everglades Place Names Card File*. Everglades National Park Archives.

[45] Tebeau, Charlton W. *Man in the Everglades*. University of Miami Press. Miami, FL. 1968. Pg. 88.

[46] Storter, Rob, with Betty Savidge Briggs, ed. *Crackers in the Glade: Life and Times in the Old Everglades.* University of Georgia Press. Athens, GA. 2000. pg. 69.

[47] Tebeau, Charlton W. *Man in the Everglades*. University of Miami Press. Miami, FL. 1968. Pg. 32.

[48] Brookfield, Charles M. & Oliver Griswold. *They All Called it Tropical*. Historical Association of Southern Florida. Miami, FL. 1949. Pg. 14.

[49] Tebeau, Charlton W. *Man in the Everglades*. University of Miami Press. Miami, FL. 1968. Pg. 27.

[50] Wood, Jimmie. Interview, 1985. *Everglades Place Names Card File*. Everglades National Park Archives.

[51] Maxwell, Ralph. Interview, 1968. *Everglades Place Names Card File*. Everglades National Park Archives.

[52] Simmons, Glen & Laura Ogden. *Gladesmen: Gator Hunters, Moonshiners, and Skiffers*. University Press of Florida. Gainesville, FL. 1998. Pg. 147.

[53] Stokes, Gordon. "Chatham". *Encyclopedia Americana*. Grolier Online, 2005. http://go.grolier.com (July 17, 2005).

[54] Brown, Peter Douglas. "Pitt, William, the Elder". *Encyclopedia Americana*. Grolier Online, 2005. http://go.grolier.com.

[55] Romans, Bernard. *A Concise Natural History of East and West Florida*. 1775. Reprinted by Pelican Publishing Company. New Orleans, LA. 1998. Pg. 279.

[56] Tebeau, Charlton W. *Florida's Last Frontier*. University of Miami Press. Miami, FL. 1957. Pg. 41.

[57] Buker, George E. *Swamp Sailors in the Second Seminole War*. University Press of Florida. Gainesville, FL. 1997. Pg. 9-10.

[58] Brookfield, Charles M. & Oliver Griswold. *They All Called it Tropical*. Historical Association of Southern Florida. Miami, FL. 1949. Pg. 52-55.

[59] Robertson, William B., Jr. "Ornithology of The Cruise of the Bonton". *Tequesta: The Journal of Historical Association of Southern Florida*. 1962. No. 22.

EVERGLADES NATIONAL PARK

[60] Pierce, Charles William. "The Cruise of the Bonton". *Tequesta: The Journal of Historical Association of Southern Florida.* 1962. No. 22.

[61] Tebeau, Charlton W. *Man in the Everglades.* University of Miami Press. Miami, FL. 1968. Pgs. 89-93.

[62] Tebeau, Charlton W. *The Story of Chokoloskee Bay Country.* Florida Flair Books. Miami, FL. 1955. Pgs. 5-6.

[63] Brookfield, Charles Mann. Interview by Love Dean. Early 1982. Islamorada Branch, Monroe Public Library. Later printed as an article for *Florida Keys Magazine*, First Quarter, 1982.

[64] Tebeau, Charlton W. *Man in the Everglades.* University of Miami Press. Miami, FL. 1968. Pg. 159-160.

[65] *Everglades Place Names Card File.* Everglades National Park Archives. 1958-1985.

[66] Gilpin, Vincent. *The Cruise of the Seminole Among the Florida Keys.* Published by the Gilpin Family. 2000.

[67] *Everglades Place Names Card File.* Everglades National Park Archives. 1958-1985.

[68] Storter, Rob, with Betty Savidge Briggs, ed. *Crackers in the Glade: Life and Times in the Old Everglades.* University of Georgia Press. Athens, GA. 2000. pgs. 82-82

[69] Moore, Joseph Curtis. "Raccoon Parade". *Everglades Natural History.* Everglades Natural History Association. 1953. Pg. 119.

[70] Tebeau, Charlton W. *Man in the Everglades.* University of Miami Press. Miami, FL. 1968. Pg. 164.

[71] Simmons, Glen & Laura Ogden. *Gladesmen: Gator Hunters, Moonshiners, and Skiffers.* University Press of Florida. Gainesville, FL. 1998. Pg. 133.

[72] Simmons, Glen & Laura Ogden. *Gladesmen: Gator Hunters, Moonshiners, and Skiffers.* University Press of Florida. Gainesville, FL. 1998. Pg. 133.

[73] Kale, Herbert W., II & David S. Maehr. *Florida Birds: A Handbook and Reference.* Pineapple Press. Sarasota, FL. 1990. Pg. 36-37.

[74] *Everglades Place Names Card File.* Everglades National Park Archives. 1958-1985.

[75] *Everglades Place Names Card File.* Everglades National Park Archives. 1958-1985.

[76] Kale, Herbert W., II & David S. Maehr. *Florida Birds: A Handbook and Reference.* Pineapple Press. Sarasota, FL. 1990. Pg. 67.

[77] Brown, Loren G. "Totch". *Totch: A Life in the Everglades.* University Press of Florida. Gainesville, FL. 1993. Pg. 33.

[78] Pierce, Charles William. "The Cruise of the Bonton". *Tequesta: The Journal of Historical Association of Southern Florida.* 1962. No. 22.

[79] Storter, Rob, with Betty Savidge Briggs, ed. *Crackers in the Glade: Life and Times in the Old Everglades.* University of Georgia Press. Athens, GA. 2000. pg. 39.

[80] Brown, Loren G. "Totch". *Totch: A Life in the Everglades.* University Press of Florida. Gainesville, FL. 1993. Pg. 49.

[81] Moore, Joseph Curtis. "A Story of Cuthbert Rookery". *Everglades Natural History*. Everglades Natural History Association. 1953. Pg. 182.

[82] McCally, David. *The Everglades: An Environmental History*. University Press of Florida, 1999. Pg. 79.

[83] United States Fish and Wildlife Service. *Florida Atlas of Breeding Sites for Herons and Their Allies: 1976-78*. August 1982.

[84] Taylor, Jean. *The Villages of South Dade*. Byron Kennedy and Company. St. Petersburg, FL. 1985. Pg. 224.

[85] Tebeau, Charlton W. *Man in the Everglades*. University of Miami Press. Miami, FL. 1968. Pg. 96.

[86] Tebeau, Charlton W. *Man in the Everglades*. University of Miami Press. Miami, FL. 1968. Pg. 163.

[87] Moore, Joseph Curtis. "A Mound on a Key in Florida Bay". *Everglades Natural History*. Everglades Natural History Association. 1953. Pg. 67-68.

[88] Davison, Ann. *Florida Junket*. Peter Davies, Ltd. London, England. 1964.

[89] Derr, Mark. *Some Kind of Paradise: A Chronicle of Man and the Land in Florida*. University Press of Florida. Gainesville, FL. 1998. Pg. 101.

[90] Simpson, Charles Torrey. *Out of Doors in Florida: The Adventures of a Naturalist, Together with Essays on the Wild Life and the Geology of the State*. E.B. Douglas Company. Miami, FL. 1923. Pg. 110.

[91] Dimock, A.W. & Julian A. *Florida Enchantments*. The Outing Publishing Company. New York. 1908. Reprint 1975.

[92] Cruickshank, Helen G. *Flight Into Sunshine: Bird Experiences in Florida*. The Macmillan Company. New York. 1948. Pg. 118.

[93] Wunderlin, Richard P. *Guide to the Vascular Plants of Florida*. University Press of Florida. Gainesville, FL. 1998. Pg. 446.

[94] Small, John Kunkel. "Historic Trails, by Land and by Water". *Journal of the New York Botanical Garden*. 22: 193-222. 1921. Pg. 215.

[95] National Park Service. *Bird Checklist of Everglades National Park*. 2005.

[96] Tebeau, Charlton W. *Man in the Everglades*. University of Miami Press. Miami, FL. 1968. Pg. 31.

[97] Tebeau, Charlton W. *Man in the Everglades*. University of Miami Press. Miami, FL. 1968. Pg. 30.

[98] Wood, Jimmie. Interview, 1985. *Everglades Place Names Card File*. Everglades National Park Archives.

[99] Hammer, Roger Lee. *Personal Commentary*. 2004.

[100] Kale, Herbert W., II & David S. Maehr. *Florida Birds: A Handbook and Reference*. Pineapple Press. Sarasota, FL. 1990. Pg. 56.

[101] National Park Service. *Bird Checklist of Everglades National Park*. 2005.

[102] Tebeau, Charlton W. *Man in the Everglades*. University of Miami Press. Miami, FL. 1968. Pg. 137.

[103] Morgan, Curtis. "Man's Hand Evident as Sea Washes Away Fragile Shoreline". *Miami Herald*. Sunday, May 15, 2005.

[104] Will, Lawrence E. *A Dredgeman of Cape Sable*. The Glades Historical Society. Belle Glade, FL. 1968. Pg. 87.

[105] National Park Service. *Mammals of Everglades National Park*.

[106] Simmons, Glen & Laura Ogden. *Gladesmen: Gator Hunters, Moonshiners, and Skiffers*. University Press of Florida. Gainesville, FL. 1998. Pg. 146.

[107] Brookfield, Charles Mann. Interview by Love Dean. Early 1982. Islamorada Branch, Monroe Public Library. Later printed as an article for *Florida Keys Magazine*, First Quarter, 1982.

[108] Hammer, Roger L. *Everglades National Park and the Surrounding Area; A Guide to Exploring the Great Outdoors*. Globe Pequot Press. Guilford, CT. 2005.

[109] Tebeau, Charlton W. *Man in the Everglades*. University of Miami Press. Miami, FL. 1968. Pg. 142.

[110] Beard, Daniel B. *Everglades National Park Project*. National Park Service. United States Department of the Interior. 1938. Pgs. 76-77.

[111] Allen, Robert P. "Comments on the Status of the Flamingo in Florida". *Everglades Natural History*. Everglades Natural History Association. June 1954. Vol. 2 No. 2. Pg. 115.

[112] Bloodworth, Bertha Ernestine. *Florida Place-Names*. University of Florida. August 1959. Pg. 113.

[113] Will, Lawrence E. *A Dredgeman of Cape Sable*. The Glades Historical Society. Belle Glade, FL. 1968. Pg. 50.

[114] Ross, Carl. Interview, 1968. *Everglades Place Names Card File*. Everglades National Park Archives.

[115] Utley, Robert M. & Barry Mackintosh. *The Department of Everything Else: Highlights of Interior History*. Department of Interior. 1989.

[116] Tebeau, Charlton W. *Man in the Everglades*. University of Miami Press. Miami, FL. 1968. Pg. 77-78.

[117] Tebeau, Charlton W. *Man in the Everglades*. University of Miami Press. Miami, FL. 1968. Pg. 101.

[118] Stokes, Richard. *Everglades Place Names Card File*. Everglades National Park Archives. 1958-1986.

[119] Tebeau, Charlton W. *Man in the Everglades*. University of Miami Press. Miami, FL. 1968. Pg. 118.

[120] Maxwell, Ralph. Interview, 1968. *Everglades Place Names Card File*. Everglades National Park Archives.

[121] Brookfield, Charles M. & Oliver Griswold. *They All Called it Tropical*. Historical Association of Southern Florida. Miami, FL. 1949. Pgs. 52-55.

EVERGLADES NATIONAL PARK

[122] Maxwell, Ralph. Interview, 1968. *Everglades Place Names Card File.* Everglades National Park Archives.

[123] Simmons, Glen & Laura Ogden. *Gladesmen: Gator Hunters, Moonshiners, and Skiffers.* University Press of Florida. Gainesville, FL. 1998. Pg. 52.

[124] Simmons, Glen. *Everglades Place Names Card File.* Everglades National Park Archives. 1958-1985.

[125] Simmons, Glen & Laura Ogden. *Gladesmen: Gator Hunters, Moonshiners, and Skiffers.* University Press of Florida. Gainesville, FL. 1998. Pg. 177.

[126] National Park Service. *History of Hidden Lake.* Everglades National Park Archives.

[127] Tebeau, Charlton W. *Man in the Everglades.* University of Miami Press. Miami, FL. 1968. Pg. 111.

[128] Tebeau, Charlton W. *Man in the Everglades.* University of Miami Press. Miami, FL. 1968. Pg. 106-107.

[129] Paige, John C. *Historic Resource Study for Everglades National Park.* National Park Service. 1986. Pgs. 146-147.

[130] Brown, Loren G. "Totch". *Totch: A Life in the Everglades.* University Press of Florida. Gainesville, FL. 1993. Pg. 59.

[131] Brown, Loren G. "Totch". *Totch: A Life in the Everglades.* University Press of Florida. Gainesville, FL. 1993. Pg. 45.

[132] Stone, Maria. *The Tamiami Trail: A Collection of Stories.* Butterfly Press. Naples, FL. 1998. Pg. 34.

[133] Storter, Rob, with Betty Savidge Briggs, ed. *Crackers in the Glade: Life and Times in the Old Everglades.* University of Georgia Press. Athens, GA. 2000. pg. 86.

[134] Dickinson, W. E. "In Quest of An Adult Crocodile". *Everglades Natural History.* Everglades Natural History Association. December 1953. Vol. 1, No. 4.

[135] Simmons, Glen & Laura Ogden. *Gladesmen: Gator Hunters, Moonshiners, and Skiffers.* University Press of Florida. Gainesville, FL. 1998. Pg. 172.

[136] Saunders, Gene. Interview, 1968. *Everglades Place Names Card File.* Everglades National Park Archives. Homestead, FL.

[137] Ross, Carl. Interview, 1968. *Everglades Place Names Card File.* Everglades National Park Archives.

[138] Maxwell, Ralph. Interview, 1968. *Everglades Place Names Card File.* Everglades National Park Archives.

[139] Tebeau, Charlton W. *Florida's Last Frontier.* University of Miami Press. Miami, FL. 1957. Pgs.119-125.

[140] Will, Lawrence E. *A Dredgeman of Cape Sable.* The Glades Historical Society. Belle Glade, FL. 1968. Pg. 127.

[141] Brookfield, Charles Mann. Interview by Love Dean. Early 1982. Islamorada Branch, Monroe Public Library. Later printed as an article for *Florida Keys Magazine*, First Quarter, 1982.

[142] McMullen, E. Wallace, Jr. *English Topographic Terms in Florida 1563-1874*. University of Florida Press. Gainesville, FL. 1953. Pg. 142.

[143] Simmons, Glen & Laura Ogden. *Gladesmen: Gator Hunters, Moonshiners, and Skiffers*. University Press of Florida. Gainesville, FL. 1998. Pg. 175-176.

[144] Tebeau, Charlton W. *Man in the Everglades*. University of Miami Press. Miami, FL. 1968. Pgs. 125-126.

[145] Simmons, Glen & Laura Ogden. *Gladesmen: Gator Hunters, Moonshiners, and Skiffers*. University Press of Florida. Gainesville, FL. 1998. Pg. 175-176.

[146] Tebeau, Charlton W. *Man in the Everglades*. University of Miami Press. Miami, FL. 1968. Pgs. 125-126.

[147] Simmons, Glen & Laura Ogden. *Gladesmen: Gator Hunters, Moonshiners, and Skiffers*. University Press of Florida. Gainesville, FL. 1998. Pg. 29.

[148] Andrews, Allen H. *A Yank Pioneer in Florida*. Douglas Printing Co., Inc. Jacksonville, FL. 1950. Pg. 319.

[149] Brown, Loren G. "Totch". *Totch: A Life in the Everglades*. University Press of Florida. Gainesville, FL. 1993. Pg. 11.

[150] Tebeau, Charlton W. *Florida's Last Frontier*. University of Miami Press. Miami, FL. 1957. Pg. 111.

[151] Tebeau, Charlton W. *Man in the Everglades*. University of Miami Press. Miami, FL. 1968. Pg. 102-103.

[152] Tebeau, Charlton W. *Man in the Everglades*. University of Miami Press. Miami, FL. 1968. Pg. 32.

[153] McCally, David. *The Everglades: An Environmental History*. University Press of Florida, 1999.

[154] Alexander, Taylor R., "The Largest Mahogany Tree". *Everglades Natural History*. Everglades Natural History Association. March 1953. Vol. 1 No. 1. Pg. 10.

[155] Will, Lawrence E. *A Dredgeman of Cape Sable*. The Glades Historical Society. Belle Glade, FL. 1968. Pg. 68.

[156] Will, Lawrence E. *A Dredgeman of Cape Sable*. The Glades Historical Society. Belle Glade, FL. 1968. Pg. 84.

[157] Pierce, Charles William. "The Cruise of the Bonton". *Tequesta: The Journal of Historical Association of Southern Florida*. 1962. No. 22.

[158] Robertson, William B., Jr. "Ornithology of the Cruise of the *Bonton*", *Tequesta: The Journal of the Historical Association of Southern Florida*, Miami, FL. 1962. No. 22.

[159] Brookfield, Charles Mann. Interview by Love Dean. Early 1982. Islamorada Branch, Monroe Public Library. Later printed as an article for *Florida Keys Magazine*, First Quarter, 1982.

[160] Buker, George E. *Swamp Sailors in the Second Seminole War*. University Press of Florida. Gainesville, FL. 1997. Pg. 97-114.

[161] McMullen, E. Wallace, Jr. *English Topographic Terms in Florida 1563-1874*. University of Florida Press. Gainesville, FL. 1953.

EVERGLADES NATIONAL PARK

[162] Brookfield, Charles Mann. Interview by Love Dean. Early 1982. Islamorada Branch, Monroe Public Library. Later printed as an article for *Florida Keys Magazine*, First Quarter, 1982.

[163] Brookfield, Charles Mann. Interview by Love Dean. Early 1982. Islamorada Branch, Monroe Public Library. Later printed as an article for *Florida Keys Magazine*, First Quarter, 1982.

[164] Tebeau, Charlton W. *Man in the Everglades*. University of Miami Press. Miami, FL. 1968. Pg. 106.

[165] Tebeau, Charlton W. *Man in the Everglades*. University of Miami Press. Miami, FL. 1968. Pgs. 155-156.

[166] Maxwell, Ralph. Interview, 1968. *Everglades Place Names Card File*. Everglades National Park Archives.

[167] Oppel, Frank & Tony Meisel. *Tales of Old Florida*. Book Sales, Inc. Secaucus, NJ. 1987. Pg. 135.

[168] Maxwell, Ralph. Interview, 1968. *Everglades Place Names Card File*. Everglades National Park Archives.

[169] Loftus, William F. "Inventory of Fishes of Everglades National Park". *Florida Scientist*. Vol. 63, No. 1, Winter 2000.

[170] Dunaway, Vic. *Florida Sportsman: Sport Fish of Florida*. Wickstrom Publishers, Inc. Miami, FL.1998.

[171] Tebeau, Charlton W. *The Story of Chokoloskee Bay Country*. Florida Flair Books. Miami, FL. 1955. Pg. 40.

[172] Brown, Loren G. "Totch". *Totch: A Life in the Everglades*. University Press of Florida. Gainesville, FL. 1993. Pg. 48.

[173] Paige, John C. *Historic Resource Study for Everglades National Park*. National Park Service. 1986. Pg. 86.

[174] Orme, Roy. Interview, 1968. *Everglades Place Names Card File*. Everglades National Park Archives.

[175] Brookfield, Charles Mann. Interview by Love Dean. Early 1982. Islamorada Branch, Monroe Public Library. Later printed as an article for *Florida Keys Magazine*, First Quarter, 1982.

[176] National Park Service. *Everglades Official Map and Guide*. 2004.

[177] Simmons, Glen & Laura Ogden. *Gladesmen: Gator Hunters, Moonshiners, and Skiffers*. University Press of Florida. Gainesville, FL. 1998. Pg. 177.

[178] Maxwell, Ralph. Interview, 1968. *Everglades Place Names Card File*. Everglades National Park Archives.

[179] Tebeau, Charlton W. *Man in the Everglades*. University of Miami Press. Miami, FL. 1968. Pg. 113.

[180] Brown, Loren G. "Totch". *Totch: A Life in the Everglades*. University Press of Florida. Gainesville, FL. 1993. Pg. 37.

EVERGLADES NATIONAL PARK

[181] Macdonald, David & Sasha Norris. *The Encyclopedia of Mammals*. Barnes and Noble Books, Inc. Italy. 2001. Pg. 808.

[182] Darwin, Arthur Leslie. *Everglades Place Names Card File*. Everglades National Park Archives. 1958-1986.

[183] Gingerich, Jerry Lee. *Florida's Fabulous Mammals*. World Publications. Tampa, FL. 1999.

[184] Dimock, A.W. & Julian A. *Florida Enchantments*. The Outing Publishing Company. New York. 1908. Reprint 1975. Pg. 289.

[185] Agassiz, Garnault. "Florida in Tomorrow's Sun". *Suniland*. November, 1925. Vol. 3, No. 2. Pgs. 37-45; 88-94; 113-133.

[186] Read, William A. *Florida Place-Names of Indian Origin and Seminole Personal Names*. Louisiana State University Press. Baton Rouge, LA. 1934. Pg. 27.

[187] Douglas, Marjory Stoneman. *The Everglades: River of Grass*. Pineapple Press. Sarasota, FL. 1947. Reprint 1997. Pg. 8.

[188] Stevenson, George B. *Trees of Everglades National Park and the Florida Keys*. Florida National Parks and Monuments Association. Homestead, FL. 1969. Revised 1992.

[189] Brookfield, Charles Mann. Interview by Love Dean. Early 1982. Islamorada Branch, Monroe Public Library. Later printed as an article for *Florida Keys Magazine*, First Quarter, 1982.

[190] Brookfield, Charles Mann. Interview by Love Dean. Early 1982. Islamorada Branch, Monroe Public Library. Later printed as an article for *Florida Keys Magazine*, First Quarter, 1982.

[191] Brookfield, Charles Mann. Interview by Love Dean. Early 1982. Islamorada Branch, Monroe Public Library. Later printed as an article for *Florida Keys Magazine*, First Quarter,1982.

[192] Stevenson, George B. *Trees of Everglades National Park and the Florida Keys*. Florida National Parks and Monuments Association. Homestead, FL. 1969. Revised 1992. Pg. 6.

[193] *Everglades Natural History*. Everglades Natural History Association. March 1953. Vol. 1 No.1. Pg. 5.

[194] Beater, Jack. *Pirates and Buried Treasure on Florida Islands, Including the Gasparilla Story*. Great Outdoors Publishing. St. Petersburg, FL. 1959. Pg. 27-33.

[195] Saunders, Gene. Interview, 1968. *Everglades Place Names Card File*. Everglades National Park Archives.

[196] Maxwell, Ralph. Interview, 1968. *Everglades Place Names Card File*. Everglades National Park Archives.

[197] Faye, Shirley. *Everglades Place Names Card File*. Everglades National Park Archives. 1958-1986.

[198] Devlin, John C. & Grace Naismith. *The World of Roger Tory Peterson*. New York Times Books. New York, NY. 1977.

EVERGLADES NATIONAL PARK

[199] Allen, Robert P. *Flame Birds*. Dodd, Mead & Co, New York, NY. 1942.

[200] *Everglades Place Names Card File*. Everglades National Park Archives. 1958-1986.

[201] Brown, Loren G. "Totch". *Totch: A Life in the Everglades*. University Press of Florida. Gainesville, FL. 1993. Pg. 37.

[202] National Park Service. *Bird Checklist of Everglades National Park*. 2005.

[203] Andrews, Allen H. *A Yank Pioneer in Florida*. Douglas Printing Co., Inc. Jacksonville, FL. 1950. Pg. 295.

[204] Kale, Herbert W., II & David S. Maehr. *Florida Birds: A Handbook and Reference*. Pineapple Press. Sarasota, FL. 1990.

[205] Brookfield, Charles Mann. Interview by Love Dean. Early 1982. Islamorada Branch, Monroe Public Library. Later printed as an article for *Florida Keys Magazine*, First Quarter, 1982.

[206] Macdonald, David & Sasha Norris. *The Encyclopedia of Mammals*. Barnes and Noble Books, Inc. Italy. 2001. Pg. 220-239.

[207] *Everglades Place Names Card File*. Everglades National Park Archives. 1958-1986.

[208] *Everglades Place Names Card File*. Everglades National Park Archives. 1958-1986.

[209] Maxwell, Ralph. Interview, 1968. *Everglades Place Names Card File*. Everglades National Park Archives.

[210] Will, Lawrence E. *A Dredgeman of Cape Sable*. The Glades Historical Society. Belle Glade, FL. 1968. Pg. 50.

[211] Tebeau, Charlton W. *Man in the Everglades*. University of Miami Press. Miami, FL. 1968. Pg. 149.

[212] *Everglades Place Names Card File*. Everglades National Park Archives. 1958-1986.

[213] Tebeau, Charlton W. *Florida's Last Frontier*. University of Miami Press. Miami, FL. 1957. Pg. 45.

[214] Beard, Daniel B. *Everglades National Park Project*. National Park Service. United States Department of the Interior. 1938. Pg. 40.

[215] Brookfield, Charles Mann. Interview by Love Dean. Early 1982. Islamorada Branch, Monroe Public Library. Later printed as an article for *Florida Keys Magazine*, First Quarter, 1982.

[216] *Everglades Place Names Card File*. Everglades National Park Archives. 1958-1986.

[217] Brookfield, Charles Mann. Interview by Love Dean. Early 1982. Islamorada Branch, Monroe Public Library. Later printed as an article for *Florida Keys Magazine*, First Quarter, 1982.

[218] Hammer, Roger L. *Florida Keys Wildflowers*. Globe Pequot Press. Guilford, CT. 2004

[219] Koehler, P. G. & F. M. Oi. *Biting Flies*. Florida Cooperative Extension Service, Institute of Food and Agricultural Sciences, University of Florida. April 1991. Revised April 2003.

[220] Tebeau, Charlton W. *The Story of Chokoloskee Bay Country*. Florida Flair Books. Miami, FL. 1955. Pgs. 39-40.

[221] Tebeau, Charlton W. *Florida's Last Frontier*. University of Miami Press. Miami, FL. 1966. pg. 112.

[222] Pierce, Charles William. "The Cruise of the Bonton". *Tequesta: The Journal of Historical Association of Southern Florida*. 1962. No. 22.

[223] Tebeau, Charlton W. *The Story of Chokoloskee Bay Country*. Florida Flair Books. Miami, FL. 1955. Pg. 41.

[224] Maxwell, Ralph. Interview, 1968. *Everglades Place Names Card File*. Everglades National Park Archives.

[225] Will, Lawrence E. *A Dredgeman of Cape Sable*. The Glades Historical Society. Belle Glade, FL. 1968. Pg. 69.

[226] Tebeau, Charlton W. *Man in the Everglades*. University of Miami Press. Miami, FL. 1968. Pg. 164.

[227] Grey, Zane. *Tales of Southern Rivers*. Harper & Brothers Publishers. New York, NY. 1924. Pg. 54.

[228] Willoughby, Hugh L. *Across the Everglades*. Florida Classics Library. Port Selerno, FL. 1898. Pg. 98.

[229] Loftus, William F. *Personal Commentary*. June 3, 2005.

[230] Loftus, William F. "Inventory of Fishes of Everglades National Park". *Florida Scientist*. Vol. 63, No. 1, Winter 2000. Pg. 32.

[231] Davison, Ann. *Florida Junket*. Peter Davies, Ltd. London, England. 1964.

[232] Brookfield, Charles Mann. Interview by Love Dean. Early 1982. Islamorada Branch, Monroe Public Library. Later printed as an article for *Florida Keys Magazine*, First Quarter, 1982.

[233] Brookfield, Charles M. & Oliver Griswold. *They All Called it Tropical*. Historical Association of Southern Florida. Miami, FL. 1949. Pg. 40.

[234] Willoughby, Hugh L. *Across the Everglades*. Florida Classics Library. Port Selerno, FL. 1898. Pg. 83-88.

[235] Jumper, Betty Mae. *Seminole Legends*. Pineapple Press. Sarasota, FL.

[236] Tebeau, Charlton W. *The Story of Chokoloskee Bay Country*. Florida Flair Books. Miami, FL. 1955.

[237] Dimock, A.W. & Julian A. *Florida Enchantments*. The Outing Publishing Company. New York. 1908. Reprint 1975.

[238] Tennant, Alan. *A Field Guide to Snakes of Florida*. Gulf Publishing Company. Houston, TX. 1997.

[239] Donnell, Marianne. *Toponyms of Florida: Decisions 1890-1976 plus 1977 addendum*. University Presses of Florida. Gainesville, FL. 1978.

[240] Tebeau, Charlton W. *Florida's Last Frontier*. University of Miami Press. Miami, FL. 1966. Pgs. 115-117.

[241] Storter, Rob, with Betty Savidge Briggs, ed. *Crackers in the Glade: Life and Times in the Old Everglades.* University of Georgia Press. Athens, GA. 2000.

[242] Andrews, Allen H. *A Yank Pioneer in Florida.* Douglas Printing Co., Inc. Jacksonville, FL. 1950. Pg. 80.

[243] Brown, Loren G. "Totch". *Totch: A Life in the Everglades.* University Press of Florida. Gainesville, FL. 1993. Pg. 17.

[244] Brown, Loren G. "Totch". *Totch: A Life in the Everglades.* University Press of Florida. Gainesville, FL. 1993. Pg. 36.

[245] Brown, Loren G. "Totch". *Totch: A Life in the Everglades.* University Press of Florida. Gainesville, FL. 1993. Pg. 34.

[246] Oppel, Frank & Tony Meisel. *Tales of Old Florida.* Book Sales, Inc. Secaucus, NJ. 1987. Pg. 12.

[247] Bloodworth, Bertha Ernestine. *Florida Place-Names.* University of Florida. August 1959. Pg. 21.

[248] Simmons, Glen. *Everglades Place Names Card File.* Everglades National Park Archives. 1958-1986.

[249] Grey, Zane. *Tales of Southern Rivers.* Harper & Brothers Publishers. New York, NY. 1924. Pg. 85.

[250] Robertson, William B., Jr. *Birds of Everglades National Park.* National Park Service. 1984.

[251] Brookfield, Charles Mann. Interview by Love Dean. Early 1982. Islamorada Branch, Monroe Public Library. Later printed as an article for *Florida Keys Magazine*, First Quarter, 1982.

[252] Meshaka, Walter E., William F. Loftus, & Todd Steiner. The Herpetofauna of Everglades National Park. *Florida Scientist.* Spring 2000. Vol. 63, No. 2.

[253] Ashton, Ray E. & Patricia Sawyer Ashton. *Handbook of Reptiles and Amphibians of Florida Part Two: Lizards, Turtles & Crocodilians.* Windward Publishing, Inc. Miami, FL. 1985. Pg. 142.

[254] McMullen, E. Wallace, Jr. *English Topographic Terms in Florida 1563-1874.* University of Florida Press. Gainesville, FL. 1953. Pg. 96.

[255] Brown, Loren G. "Totch". *Totch: A Life in the Everglades.* University Press of Florida. Gainesville, FL. 1993. Pg. 166.

[256] *Everglades Place Names Card File.* Everglades National Park Archives. 1958-1986.

[257] Brookfield, Charles Mann. Interview by Love Dean. Early 1982. Islamorada Branch, Monroe Public Library. Later printed as an article for *Florida Keys Magazine*, First Quarter, 1982.

[258] Brookfield, Charles Mann. Interview by Love Dean. Early 1982. Islamorada Branch, Monroe Public Library. Later printed as an article for *Florida Keys Magazine*, First Quarter, 1982.

[259] Dimock, A.W. & Julian A. *Florida Enchantments.* The Outing Publishing Company. New York. 1908. Reprint 1975. Pg. 227-228.

[260] Loftus, William F. "Inventory of Fishes of Everglades National Park". *Florida Scientist*. Vol. 63, No. 1, Winter 2000.

[261] Brown, Loren G. "Totch". *Totch: A Life in the Everglades*. University Press of Florida. Gainesville, FL. 1993. Pg. 7.

[262] Tebeau, Charlton W. *The Story of Chokoloskee Bay Country*. Florida Flair Books. Miami, FL. 1955. Pgs. 8-9.

[263] Brown, Loren G. "Totch". *Totch: A Life in the Everglades*. University Press of Florida. Gainesville, FL. 1993. Pg. 8.

[264] Saunders, Gene. Interview, 1968. *Everglades Place Names Card File*. Everglades National Park Archives.

[265] Tebeau, Charlton W. *Man in the Everglades*. University of Miami Press. Miami, FL. 1968. Pg. 86-87.

[266] Storter, Rob, with Betty Savidge Briggs, ed. *Crackers in the Glade: Life and Times in the Old Everglades*. University of Georgia Press. Athens, GA. 2000. Pg. 67.

[267] Burnett, Gene M. *Florida's Past, People and Events that Shaped the State: Volume 1*. Pineapple Press. Sarasota, FL. 1986. Pg. 98.

[268] Tebeau, Charlton W. *Man in the Everglades*. University of Miami Press. Miami, FL. 1968. Pg. 88.

[269] Burnett, Gene M. *Florida's Past, People and Events that Shaped the State: Volume 1*. Pineapple Press. Sarasota, FL. 1986. Pg. 98.

[270] Simmons, Glen & Laura Ogden. *Gladesmen: Gator Hunters, Moonshiners, and Skiffers*. University Press of Florida. Gainesville, FL. 1998. Pg. 138.

[271] Tebeau, Charlton W. *Man in the Everglades*. University of Miami Press. Miami, FL. 1968. Pg. 137.

[272] Tebeau, Charlton W. *Man in the Everglades*. University of Miami Press. Miami, FL. 1968. Pg. 164.

[273] *Everglades Place Names Card File*. Everglades National Park Archives. 1958-1986.

[274] Motte, Jacob Rhett. *Journey Into Wilderness*. University of Florida Press. Gainesville, FL. 1853. Reprint 1963. Pg. 236.

[275] Moore, Joseph Curtis. "A Mound on a Key in Florida Bay". *Everglades Natural History*. Everglades Natural History Association. 1953. Pg. 70.

[276] Wood, Jimmie. Interview, 1985. *Everglades Place Names Card File*. Everglades National Park Archives.

[277] Davison, Ann. *Florida Junket*. Peter Davies, Ltd. London, England. 1964. Pg. 98.

[278] Read, William A. *Florida Place-Names of Indian Origin and Seminole Personal Names*. Louisiana State University Press. Baton Rouge, LA. 1934. Pg. 40.

[279] *Everglades Place Names Card File*. Everglades National Park Archives. 1958-1986.

[280] Tebeau, Charlton W. *The Story of Chokoloskee Bay Country*. Florida Flair Books. Miami, FL. 1955. Pg. 48.

Further Reading

Andrews, Allen H. *A Yank Pioneer in Florida.* Douglas Printing Co., Inc. Jacksonville, FL. 1950.

Brookfield, Charles M. & Oliver Griswold. *They All Called it Tropical.* Historical Association of Southern Florida. Miami, FL. 1949.

Brown, Loren G. "Totch". *Totch; A Life in the Everglades.* University Press of Florida. Gainesville, FL. 1993.

Buker, George E. *Swamp Sailors in the Second Seminole War.* University Press of Florida. Gainesville, FL. 1997.

De Brahm, John Gerard William. *The Atlantic Pilot.* T. Spilsbury. London, England. 1772. Reprint 1974.

Dimock, A.W. & Julian A. *Florida Enchantments.* The Outing Publishing Company. New York. 1908. Reprint 1975.

Douglas, Marjory Stoneman. *The Everglades: River of Grass.* Pineapple Press. Sarasota, FL. 1947. Reprint 1997.

Fritchey, John. *Everglades Journal.* Florida Heritage Press. Miami, FL. 1992.

Landrum, L. Wayne. *Fort Jefferson and the Dry Tortugas National Park.* Wayne Landrum. Big Pine Key, FL. 2003.

Oppel, Frank & Tony Meisel. *Tales of Old Florida.* Book Sales, Inc. Secaucus, NJ. 1987.

Read, William A. *Florida Place-Names of Indian Origin and Seminole Personal Names.* Louisiana State University Press. Baton Rouge, LA. 1934.

Reid, Thomas. *America's Fortress; A History of Fort Jefferson, Dry Tortugas, Florida.* University Press of Florida. Gainesville, FL. 2006.

Repko, Marya. *A Brief History of the Everglades City Area.* ECity Publishing. Everglades City, FL. 2005.

Robertson, William B., Jr. *Everglades; The Park Story.* Florida National Parks and Monuments Association. Miami, FL. 1989.

Romans, Bernard. *A Concise Natural History of East and West Florida. 1775.* Pelican Publishing, New Orleans, LA. reprint 1961.

Further Reading

Simmons, Glen & Laura Ogden. *Gladesmen: Gator Hunters, Moonshiners, and Skiffers*. University Press of Florida. Gainesville, FL. 1998.

Stone, Maria. *The Tamiami Trail; A Collection of Stories*. Butterfly Press. Naples, FL. 1998.

Storter, Rob with Betty Savidge Briggs, ed. *Crackers in the Glade; Life and Times in the Old Everglades*. University of Georgia Press, Atlanta, GA. 2000.

Tebeau, Charlton W. *Florida's Last Frontier; A History of Collier County*. University of Miami Press. Miami, FL. 1966.

Tebeau, Charlton W. *Man in the Everglades*. University of Miami Press. Miami, FL. 1968.

Tebeau, Charlton W. *The Story of Chokoloskee Bay Country*. Florida Flair Books. Miami, FL. 1976.

Will, Lawrence E. *A Dredgeman of Cape Sable*. The Glades Historical Society. Belle Glade, FL. 1968.

Willoughby, Hugh L. *Across the Everglades*. Florida Classics Library. Port Salerno, FL. 1898. Reprint.